We All Do Better

Economic Priorities
For a Land of Opportunity

We All Do Better

Economic Priorities
For a Land of Opportunity

By David Bly

Fua,
Congrats on your
election to the MN House

Text design by Connie Kuhnz

Composition by Bookmobile Design and Digital Publisher Services,
Minneapolis, MN

Levins Publishing

For individual online orders go to: www.WeAllDoBetter.com

Bookstores and bulk orders contact Levins Publishing at:

info@LevinsPublishing.com

978-0-9853972-9-6

LCCN 2016930092

Union Printed in the United States

 ® GCC/IBT 152-C

For Dominique, my loving wife

Acknowledgements

I am fortunate to have worked with Levins Publishing. I could not have completed this work without the continued encouragement and guidance of Richard A. Levins, the editing skill of Jane E. Dickerson, and the graphic design skills of Alexandra Erickson.

I also thank Dane Smith for his support and encouragement. The organization he leads, Growth & Justice, has addressed many of the issues I cover in this book.

Other readers who have helped me along the way include Walter Mondale, Mark Ritchie, Alice Hausman, Matt Entenza, Neil Ritchie, Michael Howard, Mike Thorsteinson, Bob Ciernia, Jim Robbns, Ryan Winkler, Kevin Ristau, Kris Jacobs, Paul Thissen, and Barbara Battiste. I deeply regret any contributions I may have forgotten to mention here.

Most of all, I thank my constituents in Minnesota House District 20B for the great privilege of serving them in the Minnesota House of Representatives.

Preface

Why write a book about rebuilding our middle class society? Why worry so much about how the opportunities so many of us take for granted are evaporating before our very eyes? For me, the answer is personal. I am angry anybody's family member, let alone my wife, would have to endure the struggles of our dog-eat-dog economy. I don't want it to happen to anyone else. Not now. Not ever.

Dominique's story is not unusual. Most people reading this book will recognize at least some of it from their own experiences in a society in the process of losing its middle class. She went to college in the 1970's when a student could pay most state university college costs by working in the summer and during the school year. Her freshman year went well. That summer, she worked on a Wyoming ranch where she earned money to return to college. Later in Colorado, she met the man who would become her first husband. She delayed her college education and moved to Nebraska.

After raising two wonderful children, she returned to college and earned a degree in French Language and literature in order to become a French teacher. In addition to work-study, this time she borrowed money to complete her schooling. She never wanted to take a loan, but the policy balance was already tilting toward tax cuts and tilting away from keeping college affordable for all. After graduation, she faced the Board of Teaching exam. All candidates had to pass a college level math test, whether they would ever teach math or not. At this point, Dominique discovered she had a math disability. Even after several attempts and the help of excellent tutors working with her, she was unable to pass the exam.

She finally accepted that she would have to give up her dream to teach French. "In all the tests I took, I never once was tested in French, the subject that I would actually be teaching," she says. Although she was able to individually tutor students in French, that avenue didn't offer the pay and benefits of a regular teaching job. To supplement her income, she took work in a variety of vocations. She and her husband struggled at times, but owned a home, raised their kids, and felt moderately successful. As time went on, however, they grew apart and eventually divorced.

Now single, she decided to follow another long-time interest and pursue a career in the food industry by working for a variety of catering businesses. She wrote a food column for the local paper and felt ready to pursue a new adventure. She decided to sell the house, take what remained after the mortgage was settled, and study at the Culinary Institute of Arts in San Francisco. Her employer thought it was a sound idea and encouraged her. She checked into loans for school and planned to live on the money from the sale of the house while completing her studies. She secured what appeared to be a good loan, and the school promised to help her find well-paying work so she could pay off the loan after graduation.

When Domique felt everything was in order, she packed and drove off to California. After she found a small apartment, she went to register for her classes, where her excitement turned to disappointment. The registrar told her the loan she had signed up for and the school assured her was approved was no longer available. For reasons that were not made clear, she didn't qualify for the loan. "Had I not driven all that way and made down payment on an apartment, I could have been saved from what was to come.

"I didn't realize what a difference choosing a for-profit school would make in my future. I don't mean to criticize the instruction I got or most of the people I worked with, but that moment of bait and switch felt horrible. The registrar told me all I needed to do was take a loan from Sallie Mae. I knew from the terms it wasn't a good deal, which is why I chose the original loan in the first place. I wondered if I could finance my education with a credit card. The interest rate was about the same."

Not sure what to do, she was finally persuaded by the promise the school made to help her find gainful employment upon graduation. Against her better judgment, she accepted the loan. It wasn't an easy time, counting every penny, cutting back on food and other expenditures, but the promise of education for work she knew she would love kept her going. She did very well, eagerly learned skills to become a pastry chef, and anxiously looked forward to working in her new vocation.

It was not to be. The school said it didn't mean it promised to find their graduates work; they were just reporting that job prospects looked promising. Dominique discovered that starting pay for pastry chefs wouldn't pay her bills. She found a job at a Starbucks making lattes. For six months, she did self-funded tryouts in which she brought all ingredients and created desserts for restaurant owners while they watched and tasted. She worked hard, lived on next to nothing, and had little to show for it. Worse yet, the loans were coming due.

She thought about going back to Nebraska and seeing if she

could get back her old catering job. Maybe she could get a raise now that she had gotten the education. But back in Lincoln her old boss had just hired a pastry chef and couldn't afford two. At the same time, she heard from a friend who had moved to Minnesota that the possibilities for working women would be much better there. She did some research and decided to move to Minnesota if she could find work.

An opportunity emerged when she heard that D'Amico's Caterers had gotten a contract to cater the Republican National Convention in St. Paul in 2008. They needed pastry chefs to help prepare thousands of elephant-shaped desserts. It seemed like just the opening she was looking for and would allow her at last to show off the great skills she had learned. You may remember that in 2008 two extreme events were about to unfold that would create a wrinkle in Dominique's plans. The first was a hurricane that drastically cut attendance at the convention, and the demand for catering was cut back. Damico's was forced to lay off workers. The second event came in the form of a major recession; job losses multiplied as the economy dried up.

Dominique found herself in a desperate situation. She had spent all of her reserves to get to Minnesota, lost her job, and had to beg Sallie Mae to defer her loans. The deferment was granted, but at the cost of added fees, increased interest, and conditions that would most likely assure she would never be able to pay off the loan. In addition, she began to get calls from Sallie Mae bill collectors. Five or six times a day, sometimes during working hours, sometimes at night, even on weekends, came the relentless calls scolding her and demanding payments that sometimes she'd already made. Her life became one of constant harassment to pay, pay, pay.

She survived by taking whatever work she could. She taught

herself the ropes of working as a cheese monger at a food cooperative. She became a bakery worker in a small, unventilated kitchen. She sold worm juice at the Minneapolis Garden show. She served as an assistant to a pastry chef, in addition to moonlighting as a banquet waitress. She sold clothing at a shopping mall for minimum wage without commission. She balanced as many as three jobs. She often had to negotiate among employers and co-workers so she could make the schedules work. She joined the ranks of those who couldn't afford to be sick.

She experienced hard physical labor, harsh conditions, and management styles that were often mean-spirited and bordered on abuse. She continued to do tryouts for restaurateurs at her own expense. Her recipes were sometimes stolen, and she was never compensated for the work or the products she made, which the restaurants then sold. When needed, she lived with friends and cut back more on food and sold what possessions she could. Whenever she thought she was on track to make regular payments on her loan, she'd find herself out of work or without a reliable car for commuting. Cheaper rent meant driving forty miles one-way to work.

Her dream of higher education became a nightmare of debt from which she could find no escape. Even bankruptcy couldn't shake the student loans that dogged her. She thought about opening a small cheese and chocolate shop, but where would she get the capital to get started? Moving to where the jobs were had backfired, and she felt unable to move again. She relied on help from friends and family, but wanted to make it on her own. She worked hard, long hours. She received unemployment benefits for a while, but even that small comfort was lost because her part-time employer neglected to include her tips in initially reporting to the unemployment agency. As a result, she ended up owing money and was paying for that on top of her student loan, rent, and any necessities. She prayed her car wouldn't break down, that her health would hold, and that she could endure the physically demanding jobs that offered only limited health care and low wages.

"Something is wrong with this picture," Dominque despairs. "How do I ever get ahead? No, I mean how do I ever get to the point where I can have my head above water and not feel like I am one bad tire or one knee injury away from disaster? I'm 61. At this rate I'll never retire. I'll die in my work clothes, if I still have a job. The worst of it is that my story isn't unique. Too many of the workers I know could tell similar stories."

How is it possible that things could go so wrong for her? How is it possible that so many of us know her story, either from personal experience or from relatives and friends? What must we do to restore the middle class promise of opportunity for all? Dominique and I married in 2012. It has been a time of joy and a time of struggle as we work together to recover from the roadblocks our winner-take-all economy has placed in her path. Working together. That's how we do it in our home. That's how we must do it as a nation.

The Five Foundations of a Middle Class Society

Not so long ago, the words "Land of Opportunity" really meant something for all Americans. We pretty much took it for granted that each and every one of us should have the opportunity to develop our God-given talents to reach our greatest potential. This didn't mean that everyone would choose to use that opportunity, or that anyone would be forced to use it. It did mean, however, that everyone had that opportunity. We know that we are all better off as a society when every American realizes their full potential. As the late Senator Paul Wellstone once said, "We all do better when we all do better."

Things are changing, and not for the better. All too often, we hear stories of families evicted from their homes when unemployment runs out, or senior citizens who must choose between buying groceries and life-sustaining medications, or the single mother who can't get a job because she must spend her time nursing her invalid son. We open the paper to read yet another story about the achievement gap in our schools. We watch the news and are shocked to learn that the United States is the world's leader in putting its citizens behind bars. Sometimes I find myself wondering if the blessing of a child so intelligent that he or she might one day develop a cure for cancer will be wasted because that child can't afford college.

These kinds of thing don't happen, or at least shouldn't, when there is a nationwide commitment for everyone to have what they need to develop their potential. This commitment goes beyond lip service and political speeches. It involves deliberate policies that maintain what I call a "middle class economy." A middle class economy is not one in which every single person makes a certain amount of money. Even in a middle class economy, some are rich and some are poor. But most of the people have most of the money. Most of the people can take care of themselves and fully develop their potential. Those that can't take care of themselves for any number of understandable reasons can count on the rest of us to get them through the rough spots.

Right now we are in the process of losing our middle class economy. We know this from news stories, and far too many of us know it from personal experience. This loss of our middle class economy and the resultant shift to a "winner take all" economy of rich and poor are behind most of the problems with which we struggle as a society.

The Spirit Level by Richard Wilkinson and Kate Pickett helped me see how and why this is so. The authors demonstrate in powerful terms how growing inequality is crippling both our society and our economy in ways that will make it harder to address the critical problems we face as a nation. Page after page of graphs illustrate how we have fallen behind other developed nations in the things a well-functioning economy must provide. Wilkinson and Pickett make a solid case that it is not so much the average income of a society that matters. More important is how that income is distributed. Countries that have the most equal income distribution do best on health and social indicators.

According to Wilkinson and Pickett, income inequality is related to "lower life expectancy, higher rates of infant mortality, shorter height, poor self-reported health, low birth weight, AIDS, and depression." They collected data from dozens of other rich countries on health, level of trust, mental illness, drug and alcohol addiction, life expectancy, infant mortality, teenage birth rates, obesity, children's educational performance, homicides, imprisonment, and social mobility. "What is most exciting about our research is that it shows that reducing inequality would increase the well-being and quality of life for all of us," the authors say. Today we have a choice: use public investment to reduce inequality or pay for the social harm caused by inequality.

Wilkinson and Pickett also believe: "Modern societies will depend increasingly on being creative, adaptable, inventive, well-informed, and flexible, able to respond generously to each other and to needs wherever they arise. Those are societies not in hock to the rich, in which people are driven by status insecurities, but of populations used to working together and respecting each other as equals." This, to me, is a longer version of what Wellstone said, "We all do better when we all do better." Any search for economic salvation motivated and driven by the greed of its individual participants is bound to fail.

Ours is the oldest modern democracy, but present-day policies and court decisions are undermining our basic democratic principles. Immense power has been ceded to an organized cadre of financial elites who have figured out how to buy their way into controlling our government. The past 30 years have seen two related trends: (1) an unraveling of benefits and opportunities for the vast majority of Americans, and (2) a massive increase in wealth for a handful of people. Leading economists assure us that if we don't take decisive action, we can expect more of the same. Economist Emmanuel Saez has carefully analyzed the shift toward a rich-and-poor economy. He says, "The market itself doesn't impose a limit on inequality, especially for those at the top." His partner in research, Thomas Picketty, has further documented and explained income inequality in his book *Capital in the 21st Century*. As I write this, the very wealthy are enjoying a good recovery from the recession of 2008 while the vast majority of Americans fall further behind.

Our descent from an economy that provided for all to one that provides for only a few has been no accident. Nor was it inevitable. The story of how government has gone from limiting greed to encouraging it is chronicled in several recent books, including Kim Phillips-Fein in *Invisible Hands: The Businessmen's Crusade Against the New Deal*; Paul Pierson and Jacob S. Hacker in *Winner Take All Politics*; and Hedrick Smith in *Who Stole the American Dream?* Each tells much the same story in different ways. When the Supreme Court determined that money was speech in 1976, things began to change quickly. The super-rich suddenly gained an advantage in their campaign to silence the power of people and weaken our democracy. Today, with the Supreme Court decision on the Citizen's United case, corporations are "people," and even misinformation and lies spread by these strange new "people" are protected speech.

Economic value is created by law. So it matters who writes the laws or what interests those laws serve. Similarly, the distribution of wealth and the flow of capital can flow one way or the other with the stroke of a legislator's pen. It matters what his or her core beliefs are. Property rights and the distribution of wealth can deny liberty to some just as easily as they bestow it on others. Amartya Sen, a Nobel Award winning economist, argues that hunger is not a product of the shortage of food. Instead, hungry people lack rights (the entitlement) to eat. The law decides, or as Sen puts it, "The law stands between food availability and food entitlement. Starvation deaths can reflect legality with a vengeance." We often use the words "free market" to describe our current economic system, but that system, as much as any other, rests on a set of legal rules establishing who can do what and a system to enforce those rules.

As President Franklin Roosevelt surveyed the ravages of the Great Depression and set out to do something about it, he said: "The thing that matters in any industrial system is what it does actually to human beings. . . ." In other words, our economic system must be just. The laws we put in place determine whether it is or is not just. The existing distribution of wealth and opportunity is a product of social choices. An evaluation of those policies and how they affect real people make it much harder to claim that rights should be defined by freedom from government intervention.

Chief Justice Charles Evans Hughes, who served from 1930–1941, argued that the Constitution protects "liberty in a social organization which requires the protection of law against the evils which menace the health, safety, morals and welfare of the people." Beginning with the founding of our nation, we have a rich tradition of concern for equality and protection from the abuses that wealth, poorly distributed, can bring about. Over 200 years ago, super-patriot Tom Paine advocated that public employment be utilized to assist those needing work, that a system of social security should provide for retirement at age 60, and that the state should provide funds so that poor families could educate and care for their children. In another example, the end of the Civil War saw the passage of amendments to the Constitution that banned slavery and limited the degree to which states could discriminate against their citizens. These amendments, in turn, broadened democracy and set us on a path that eventually resulted in the establishment of voting rights for blacks and women.

A middle class economy must never be taken for granted. For example, in many countries fewer than half of the people age 15 and over can read and write a short, simple statement about his or her everyday life. In others, health care is so substandard that one in ten babies will not live to see his or her first birthday. Those that do survive have a life expectancy of no more than 50 years. Only 10 percent of the roads in some countries are paved. Workers in some countries subsist on a few dollars per day. Opportunity is, for all practical purposes, nothing more than a dream for most people in these countries. In fact, as we look around the globe, we see that a middle class economy is the exception rather than the rule. Most countries have virtually no middle class. We are fortunate to have enjoyed the benefits of a middle class economy, but we must at the same time recognize that our middle class economy didn't just happen: it was built and maintained, just like a nice house or the interstate highway system must be built and maintained.

How do you build and maintain an enduring middle class economy? In my judgment, every middle class economy must be built on these five foundations:

- Quality education for everyone

- Health care for everyone

- A world-class transportation system

- Energy systems that maintain a clean and safe enviornment

- Living wages for all working people

Everyone agrees education is vitally important. Many states commit to quality education for all in their constitutions. But, too often, actions speak louder than words. College is harder to afford, increasingly results in crippling debt, and does not guarantee the job prospects it used to. Budget cuts are wreaking havoc at all levels of education.

We know that a society that can't provide health care for all its citizens is a society at risk. We hear that we have the best health care in the world, but the numbers tell us differently. Our health outcomes do not measure up to the rest of the developed world because our system, even with the advances made with the Affordable Care Act, does not assure universal access.

Prosperous economies require that goods and people can move around easily. Investment in transportation infrastructure is essential if we are to grow. These investments need to make life better for all citizens, regardless of race, gender or income level. But we aren't making the investments we need. We all feel the cost as roads, bridges, and public transportation are neglected.

Environment, energy, and land use go hand-in-hand in a middle class economy. A clean, safe environment supports good health and quality of life for everyone. Instead of moving forward on clean energy and correcting harmful practices, we continue to rely on fossil fuels and to live with the economic and environmental consequences.

The fifth foundation of a middle class economy is living wage jobs. Generations before us took for granted that hard-working Americans would share in our prosperity. We have abandoned that understanding. Wages for most Americans have flat-lined in spite of continuing pressure from the rising cost of life's essentials. In a 2014 survey by the Pew Foundation, over ten times as many respondents said their incomes were falling behind the cost of living than said they were getting ahead.

Legislators from state to state seem intent on passing bills to protect business interests at the expense of reducing worker and consumer protections. Others struggle to craft and pass bills to address various ills—from the environment to the achievement gap to childhood obesity. Neither strategy is enough to stop the erosion of our middle class economy. We need a more comprehensive approach because the foundations are so closely related in a system that results in opportunities for all. A sick person needs not only health care; he or she also needs reliable transportation to the hospital. Studies are beginning to relate the stress of living with low wages to higher demand for health care services. In my last visit to the hospital, I encountered a patient recovering from heart surgery who had to wait outside in the cold for several bus transfers so he could make his scheduled follow up appointments. Educating our children becomes more difficult when so many of them live in poverty. I'm sure you can think of other examples from your own experience of how a failure in one of the foundations leads to a failure in others.

As you study the foundations, you will also see that they have this in common: they are all "we" concepts. We all benefit when they are in place, and all suffer when they crumble. No one person is rich enough or powerful enough to provide them for everyone; it's a job we must do together. When we work together toward our common good, we grow a middle class economy. When we work against each other as individuals, we set ourselves on the road to becoming a Third World economy. As much as I hate to say it, I'm afraid that is exactly the path we are on. Think about it. Even with the Affordable Care Act, millions of us have limited access to health care. Our education system is no longer tops in the world. We rely too much on fossil fuels. Our water quality suffers from poor land use. Our roads and bridges are falling apart. Wages are going down at the same time corporate profits go up.

What can the United States do to save its middle class economy? Will we continue on a path to Third World status, or will we renew our commitment to opportunity for all of our citizens? In the following chapters, I take a closer look at each of the building blocks of a middle class economy. I examine where we have been, where we are now, and in what direction our policies have us headed. As you will see, much of what I say is about my home state of Minnesota where I serve in the State Legislature. But I'm sure you will also see that much of what I say about my home state applies just as much to yours. We are all in this together. We all need to get our state and federal spending priorities focused in a way that will make a difference. That way is the way to opportunity for all, the way to rebuilding the five foundations of our middle class economy.

Foundations:

EDUCATION

Too Many Children Left Behind

Americans have always seen education as important to progress and economic growth. Politicians give impassioned speeches touting education as the key to success. Actions speak louder than words, however, and budget cuts are taking a toll on education at all levels in spite of the speech-making and rhetoric. By arguing that we can't continue to throw money at problems, we have gradually abandoned poor children and children of color by eliminating programs targeted to their needs. Standardized tests are being used to condemn schools and blame teachers and their unions for the failure. The new focus on teachers and teacher quality is to make teachers take responsibility for the success or failure of all students, regardless of their community and home situations. Instead of looking at what resources are needed to educate all children in our country, we simply ask that teachers continue to do more with less.

Don Glines is the founder of the Mankato, Minnesota, based Wilson School, once described by *The National Observer* as the most innovative public school in America. He asked some questions we should all think about as we evaluate our educational policies: "Should lawyers tell farmers how to plow fields? Should doctors tell merchants how to sell suits? Should merchants tell students how to study? Should school board members, most of whom know little regarding learning research, tell learners how to learn?" More and more, we see control of our pedagogy falling into the hands of legislators who have little understanding of the process of learning or the diverse needs of students. Education policy by legislative process has given us mandated unfair testing, unnecessary curriculum, and one-size-fits-all learning environments shaped by the notion that all we need to do is test the kids to see if knowledge is being delivered in the right way. In my thirty-year public school teaching career, I saw first-hand how these educational policies often do more harm than good.

The unexamined reasoning of the testing advocates, steeped as they are in claims of common sense, could not be more unfounded. W. Edwards Deming is the statistician credited with reforming the Japanese manufacturing sector from one that was ridiculed by all to one that is among the most admired in the world. He did so by encouraging reorganization around attention to quality and continuous improvement principles. He said, "You must eliminate fear, identify stakeholders and build on trust." Workers must be seen as valuable assets with unique expertise and the ability to make necessary improvements. The atmosphere of high-stakes testing and linking test scores to pay in "pay for performance" schemes does just the opposite. It heightens fear, decreases trust, and devalues the knowledge and skills of teachers and administrators. We tell teachers that parents and legislators know better, that hard work and right methods should produce higher test scores. But tests only evaluate a moment in time, focused on product, whereas learning is a process that plays out over time. Tests only look at a small area of that learning process. By focusing only on the academic realm and ignoring the critical kinesthetic and affective domains, testing doesn't take into account the broad array of learning that takes place in schools. We end up seeing much of our education investment going to publishers of tests that have little to do with improving the learning of our children.

Nancy Folbre, writing in *The New York Times*, said, "Scores on standardized tests are not an accurate measure of success in later life, because they don't capture important aspects of emotional intelligence, such as self-control and ability to collaborate with others." Pressure to improve student test scores and teaching to the test diverts attention from other aspects of the curriculum that might better promote problem-solving skills. She referenced economists Bengt Holmstrom and Paul Milgrom who described the general problem of misaligned incentives in more formal terms: "Workers who are rewarded only for accomplishment of easily-measurable tasks reduce the effort devoted to other tasks." Clearly, something isn't right with the system—close to 40 percent of teachers in New York City quit after three years.

Teaching is a job with the impossible combination of increasing demands and decreasing compensation. To make matters worse, pressure on public budgets at all levels has forced layoffs and worsened working conditions. In some Texas school districts, teachers are now assigned custodial work. You might well ask how that will attract the best and the brightest. Most research shows that new teachers need support, encouragement and mentoring to become highly skilled. High-stakes assessments that force teachers to compete with each other discourage that collaboration. Little wonder, then, that most comprehensive studies of efforts to improve student achievement by rewarding teachers for student performance show minuscule, if any, positive results. The students of teachers with regular salaries do just as well as students with teachers who receive monetary incentives.

A 2011 study by Roland Fryer, a prominent Harvard economist, is a good example. Professor Fryer conducted a school-
based randomized trial in 250 New York City public schools
designed to better understand the impact of teacher incentives
on student achievement. He concluded, "I find no evidence that
teacher incentives increase student performance, attendance, or
graduation, nor do I find any evidence that the incentives change
student or teacher behavior." He also found some evidence that
teacher incentives (that is, rewarding teachers for improving
student test scores), especially in larger schools, seemed to decrease student achievement. Making teacher pay dependent on
student achievement cannot improve teacher-student relations,
especially those in large school where relationships are already
minimal and distant.

Aren't there better ways to meet the goal of educating all of
our citizens? In a May 2011 paper, *Standing on the Shoulders of
Giants*, Marc S. Tucker examined recent research that looked at
five countries far ahead of the United States in education outcomes. He reminded us that 100 years ago we borrowed from
other countries to build the education system we have today.
A comparison with Finland is apt. Finland began a process of
educational reform by establishing two over-riding principles:
(1) equality, that is, education to benefit everyone, and (2) high
performance through continuous improvement. Then they
moved on to, "How do you train really great teachers?" Instead
of emphasizing tests, the Finns started with the notions that
good teachers need strong training, they need to be guided by
excellent teachers, and they need lots of guided practice. They
also established that an environment of trust was essential for
a positive learning environment and worked hard to build trust
between teachers and students as well as between teachers and

administrators. The reforms allowed teachers and their union to drive what the new education system looked like. Entrance into teacher programs is more competitive and teacher training is subsidized through a Master's Degree. Now that the reforms are in place, Finland sits near the top in all world rankings of educational performance and spends no more per student than we do to get far better results.

These ideas of building trust instead of competition, of fully funding what needs to be done, of allowing teachers and their unions to take leadership roles—they make so much sense, don't they? And, yet, here in America, our policies drive us in the opposite direction. Our results, too, are headed in the opposite direction. Perhaps this is what we should expect. As the old saying goes, "You get what you pay for." Too often politicians are only willing to meet the needs of students half way, and even then only after forcing advocates to constantly justify the importance of providing what they need.

Take, for example, the field in which I have spent much of my career, special education. Since its passage in the 1970s, the Individuals with Disabilities Education Act has mandated schools provide special instruction for identified students. The mandate did not come with full funding, however, and state and federal governments have not lived up to their funding promises. Without adequate funding from the states, schools have to use other funding sources to cover special education programs. This, in turn, reduces resources that otherwise would have supported regular programs. This sets up a tension between regular and special education programs that results in more pressure to deny special education services. Parents, teachers, and school boards are put in the impossibly difficult situation of deciding which students should be fully served. The obvious answer is "all of them."

The funding answer is needless anguish for students, parents, and teachers.

Some politicians say, "It's all about choices because we have limited resources." During the last 20 years or so, the American public has been constantly asked, in one way or another, to accept the idea that our education system is wasteful and inefficient. So, instead of providing needed educational funds, our schools have seen funds withheld and have been forced to shoulder costly accountability measures such as the "No Child Left Behind" (NCLB) initiative. These misguided measures essentially assure the failure of schools. Had the NCLB program lived up to its title, it would have solved many of the problems of our educational system. Some supporters of NCLB saw it as a way to deal with those at-risk students who fall through the cracks. The problem is that the policy proposed getting "tough" with schools and teachers to make them deliver, instead of dealing with the root of the problem: the deep inequalities in our system. If a school fails, it's given state aid to help it become successful. Once successful, however, the aid is taken away and the school must again rely on local resources. In poor districts, those resources simply are not available.

No Child Left Behind has, in fact, left too many children behind. Its scheme of high-stakes tests and school and teacher report cards is not capable of creating the reforms our system may need because it doesn't help us see the problem. I'm startled when people talk about underperforming schools and students that they don't look at the economic factors that affect student learning and interest. It is both shocking and tragic that almost half of the students in our public schools qualify for subsidized lunch programs. Often the pressure to work far outweighs an economically disadvantaged student's interest in staying in school. Many live in families where there aren't enough resources to eat well, get to school on time, and feel alert and able to do good work in school. As more and more students come from communities that are themselves economically challenged, the problems become even worse. Supportive communities fade with the loss of supportive families, and increased teacher time is spent controlling behavior. Research shows that money spent supporting early childhood education and family education would be a far better investment.

Lynn Stoddard, retired Utah educator, developed a completely different approach to educating our children called "educating for human greatness." He doesn't begin by thinking about the end of an educational career and how we can give corporate America the workers they want. Technology can change the workplace and the kinds of jobs industry needs in very short order. Instead, he thinks about the beginning of each child's learning career: who they are and what they need to know. He asks, "How can we design a school so that each child can discover who they were meant to be?" Stoddard advocates for a truly student-centered education that identifies seven major powers necessary for developing human greatness: Identity, Inquiry, Interaction, Initiative, Imagination, Intuition and Integrity. Education is not about changing the student to fit a predetermined work situation. Instead, "Our message to young people is this: *We need you—just the way you are. We need you and your talents and your experience. Find your greatness and you will find your reason for living.*" What would our schools look like if this were where we started?

The problems with our educational system don't end with high school. For many decades, the United States has been the world leader in higher education. We rank first in the number of college-educated citizens between the ages of 55 and 64. However, we've slipped to seventh in the 25 to 34 year old range. We trail economic competitors such as Canada and Japan. A major cause of the stagnation in graduation rates is the cost of attending college. The cost of public college rises beyond the reach of more Americans every year. In my home state of Minnesota, the average cost for a year at a public four-year school rose 70 percent to $12,800 in just five years. This is in part a result of the state disinvestment in state colleges. As Sharon Schmickle noted in a 2009 article, Minnesota used to have a commitment to higher education that grew through the decades, brick by brick and professor by professor. All that good work is now jeopardized. State higher education funding per full-time student dropped by 28 percent during 2000 to 2007. Students and their parents must pick up an ever-increasing share.

According to the Bureau of Labor Statistics, since 1981 college tuition has consistently increased faster than the overall inflation rate. This is often explained as "runaway costs of college," but the story is more complicated. The real story is one of a change in thinking away from a college education as a public good and more toward seeing it as an individual investment. Under this philosophy, state governments trade general funding for tuition increases. The result is higher taxes on individual students disguised as higher costs for tuition. Combined with a falling minimum wage, the problem becomes ever more difficult for students to overcome. The time-honored tradition of working one's way through college has been derailed by a combination of rising costs and the falling purchasing power of the minimum wage. It's therefore not surprising that a Public Agenda survey found that 71 percent of college drop-outs said having to work was a factor, while more than half said it was a major factor. Students have tried to make up for the wage gap with student loans; the total volume of outstanding student loans exceeds that for the nation's credit card debt. No wonder a 2011 Pew Foundation survey found that 57 percent of Americans thought higher education was not worth the price.

Some argue if everyone had equal access to a college education, it would ease our income distribution problems. Ability, not family wealth, would determine who gains the benefits of going to college. However, if only the wealthy can go to college, then college degrees will no longer be a gateway into the middle class. Instead, the colleges our taxes help fund will themselves contribute to our slow slide into a Third World income distribution. A study in the *Journal of Labor Economics* doesn't give us much to cheer about. If we divide all American families into four income groups, we would see that 75.5 percent of those students coming from the top group go to college. On the other hand, only 33.3 percent coming from the bottom group go to college. This disparity is only going to get worse. Why? The reasoning in the study is simple enough. Wealth makes it easier to go to college, and most lower- and middle-class families have most of their wealth tied up in their homes. For most of us, housing has, to put it mildly, not been the source of wealth creation it used to be.

At every stage of our educational system, our weakened middle class society is both a symptom and a problem. It is a symptom because a weakened educational system leads to a weaker middle class. It is a problem because a strong middle class is necessary to advocate for and fund an educational system that provides opportunity for all Americans. We can't hope to rebuild our educational system if we continue to rely on programs that cut budgets, demonize teachers and their unions, and blame students for system-wide economic failure. We need an entirely new approach that addresses both our educational problems and the broader problems facing the middle class that must sustain our schools and colleges. In the 2013 session, the Minnesota State Legislature addressed the trend of past underinvestment by making significant investments in education, from our youngest learners all the way to students pursuing a post-secondary degree. It takes more than financial resources to provide everyone with a high quality education. Recruiting, training and retaining talented educators to lead our classrooms are also essential. And those classrooms need to be a manageable size that allows teachers to deliver the kind of one-on-one individual attention that produces the best outcomes. Reforming our student assessment system to deliver better diagnostics earlier in a student's academic career was a key part of our progress as well. These have been small but important steps that, without public consensus, can be undermined by an election.

Major investments in Minnesota's students include preschool scholarships for over 8,000 low-income families, all-day everyday kindergarten for every child, additional funding for every school, freezing tuition at state colleges and universities for two years, and expanding state financial aid for students earning a post-secondary degree. Other modest yet vital investments include an expansion of the school lunch program for low-income students, providing free breakfast for every kindergartener, more grants for "recovery schools" that provide a safe environment for students recovering from substance abuse, better training for teachers who instruct English Language Learners and tax credits for teachers who buy classroom materials for their students.

State lawmakers paired those financial investments with policy reforms intended to build a highly educated workforce that can attract and retain the kinds of jobs that pay living wages. For example, we moved away from a failed student assessment system that left almost half of our graduates in need of remedial classes upon entering college. Instead of a single test required to graduate from high school, we implemented career and college readiness exams beginning in middle school. These exams provide parents, students, and teachers with key diagnostic information that will empower them with early planning for their career goals and success in learning. By starting career and college readiness testing when students are in middle school, parents and teachers can help them correct course before it is too late.

According to the Minnesota Department of Education, the number of English language learners has tripled during the past 20 years. Over 65,000 students whose first language is not English are currently enrolled in Minnesota schools. To improve academic outcomes among this unique population of students, we knew we had to change the mindset of viewing a non-English native language as a problem to be fixed. Instead, we began our efforts by framing non-English native languages, and the children who speak them, as assets. Using that mindset, we implemented policy reforms around four goals:

- Prioritize early parent involvement

- Prepare educators to effectively teach English language learners

- Enhance systemic and institutional focus on English language learner success

- Expand support for all English language learners, including adults.

In 2013, just 59 percent of English language learners graduated from high school, with 23 percent meeting proficiency measures in math, 17 percent in reading and just 12 percent in science. Thanks to new program directions, statewide averages on those measures in 2013 came out to 61 percent, 58 percent and 53 percent, respectively.

Of course, none of these initiatives would go far without top-notch educators leading our classrooms. We took important steps toward meeting this goal by reforming our teacher licensure system, granting temporary licensure to out-of-state teachers as they prepare for in-state licensure, better teacher evaluations, and new intensive pilot programs for teacher candidates. Last, we made progress on ensuring a safe, supportive learning environment for all students by reforming our state's anti-bullying laws, which many had considered the weakest in the nation. The "Safe and Supportive Schools Act" approved in 2014 requires all districts to establish comprehensive local policies that protect all students, define prohibited conduct, provide processes for reporting and handling of complaints, and emphasize restorative justice. It also directs Minnesota to create a School Safety Technical Assistance Council and Center, which will establish norms for prevention, intervention and support, advancement of evidence-based policy and development of resources and training.

We must never forget that what we spend on educating our young people is an investment that benefits us all, and that cutting corners on those investments hurts us all. Here are some conclusions from the report *Smart Investments in Minnesota Students* that could apply as well to any other state in our union:

> *Economists, business leaders and educators agree: Minnesota's relative prosperity over the past quarter century has been driven largely by our investment in human capital. But Minnesota faces*

major economic shifts that challenge our long-term prosperity. At the current rate we are producing students with post-secondary degrees, within two decades Minnesota will not have enough skilled working adults to sustain our economy or quality of life at the levels most of us have enjoyed.

To meet the demand for skilled workers—and to ensure families can enjoy a decent standard of living—we should, by 2020, increase by 50 percent the rate of Minnesota students who finish some type of post-secondary education.

To reach that goal, we must invest in solutions now. Each year, 10,000 high school students drop out, at a cost to the state economy of $10 billion over their lifetimes.

I am proud of the progress we are making. I am proud of the Minnesota teachers and students we are better able to serve because of new programs we have put in place. But I am also increasingly convinced that we must change our attitudes if we are to make the progress we need to make. We need to see that teachers are the solution, not the problem. We need to see that an educated population benefits all of us, not just the person getting the college degree. And we need to see that "no child left behind" is a matter of significant, thoughtful investment in our children as individual gifts to our society, and not a system of useless high-stakes tests that lead us farther and farther from our goal of rebuilding our middle class society.

Foundations:

HEALTH CARE

American Lives Are at Stake

A few years ago, I went door knocking in my district and asked this question: "What is the most pressing economic issue you face?" No matter whom I asked, farmer, small business owner, city manager, or school teacher, the answer was the same: "The availability of and the runaway cost of health insurance." President Obama took a big step toward addressing this issue with the Affordable Care Act. Even most critics of the Act can see some good in the way it insures children of college age beyond a year or two of college and provides protection from being denied coverage because of pre-existing medical conditions. At the same time, even the most ardent supporters of the Affordable Care Act admit that it will never cover all Americans. There is more work to be done.

Deep down, I suspect, we all know that our nation would be better off if everyone had access to basic health services. We know that those who have access to health care and a primary physician are less likely to have severe health problems. Those fortunate individuals get early diagnosis of problems, timely treatment, and guidance toward healthier behavior. We know that the more severe an illness or injury, the more costly it is to treat. An emergency room visit may be able to treat a badly infected tooth, which could be life threatening, but it will not provide the on-going care necessary to prevent a costly return visit for the same condition. A house fire, left unchecked, can threaten an entire community, so no fire station I know of asks for proof of insurance before they send out the trucks. In the same way, we know universal access to health care reduces the risk of untreated communicable diseases that can affect all of us, insured or not.

The obvious question is, "Why doesn't a country as wealthy as ours have universal coverage?" Is it because, as some think, that without the incentive to earn money to pay for care, people won't work as hard? Millions of Americans work hard every day to put food on the table and still can't afford or don't have access to health insurance. Many of these people haven't had a physical in years and fear that an accident or injury will bankrupt them or prevent them from getting to work to support their families. On top of that, there is an especially perverse consequence of the "high health costs provide incentives to work" argument. When businesses close because of high health insurance costs, more people are unemployed and lose the opportunity to work at all. Small business owners or farmers must sometimes put their enterprise at risk by taking another job just to get medical insurance.

Let's set aside the "why" for a minute and talk about where we are, what we could be doing, and what other countries are doing. Prior to President Obama's reform, more and more people had a tougher time getting the health care they needed. For some, double-digit increases in health insurance premiums reduced the quality of coverage and put costs for even that out of reach. Others lost their jobs and, along with those jobs, insurance altogether. Those who qualified for public benefits lived in fear of being cut off as states struggled to balance their budgets. The best solution we have so far, while imperfect, is President Obama's Affordable Care Act. Instead of being embraced for its reforms, it continues to be subject to calls for its repeal, with barely a hint of what should replace it.

Washington Post correspondent T. R. Reid tells the story of Taiwanese government officials who wanted to reform their health system. They planned to visit numerous countries in search of models to guide their efforts. Hoping to cut their trip short, they came to the United States first. What they learned, however, convinced them that the United States was the last country they wanted to imitate. The United States had great hospitals and doctors and the most advanced equipment and technology, but they also found that our system was disorganized, expensive, and that a growing number of citizens went without care. They learned that the United States had an infant mortality that was over twice the level measured for Sweden, Japan, and Norway. Eventually, the Taiwanese took the best ideas from England, France, and Canada. These countries insure everyone with a national health program.

America stands alone among industrialized nations in failing to make sure all its citizens have access to health care. Our employer-based system of insurance adds its own problems to an already bad situation. Especially in a downturn, employers are reluctant to hire more of us because of costly benefits like health insurance. The self-employed, including farmers and small businesses, are often forced to do without insurance or else find a second job in their search for benefits. The cures offered for employee-based health coverage often make matters worse. Some see reduced levels of coverage for employees as the solution; others say higher costs should be passed on to employees already pressured to work for less. Perhaps worst of all, these half-baked cures take our attention away from this central message: Our employer-based insurance system is broken.

The very idea of private health insurance is fundamentally flawed. Think about it. We, as clients, pay the insurance company for what we hope is access to health care. But private insurers make money by denying coverage, not by providing it. Private insurers promised they would make medical costs affordable. Instead, we have bloated CEO salaries, unlimited paperwork, increasing costs, and high deductibles standing in the way of coverage. Instead of a thoughtful public option available to all, proposed plans come from the insurance companies, further exacerbating the problem. Because of the once-lauded praise of Managed Care plans, budget-strapped state governments turned to insurance companies to help run public health insurance programs. Costs continued to rise even though measures were taken to reduce them.

We also have more "health savings accounts." These programs set up a bank account into which you, or your employer, make a deposit. You pay medical costs out of this account until a certain high deductible level is reached. After that, your insurance company will cover the remaining costs. Although some signs show that health savings accounts are an improvement over strictly private insurance, they have their own problems. One is that an individual must have enough income in order to make a deposit into the account or else rely on an employer to cooperate with the system. Health savings accounts also encourage underuse and discourage preventive measures. Ironically, the original justification for the plans attempted to address the reverse of this issue—if people must pay upfront for their medical costs, they will be less likely to overuse the medical system. Medical care is something we seem likely to avoid rather than overuse. We don't want to be sick if we can help it, and sometimes we don't want to know we need help.

While many of us struggle and live with the stress of not knowing whether or not we will get good health coverage and care, another group of Americans enjoys a time-tested, universal, single-payer system that provides for their health care. Those Americans are senior citizens, and the system is called Medicare. Why not simply extend this to all Americans? Doing so would give everyone access to health care and make Medicare more stable.

Some worry about the government playing God by making decisions about who does and who doesn't get care because of wait times. But who can argue that the system we have now doesn't cause some people to make difficult choices and play God? In order to reduce costs, insurance companies limit health services that patients need every day. Others worry about raising taxes to pay for universal coverage even as their paychecks are eaten by a "private tax" levied by insurance companies to cover those who use the emergency room and are unable to pay. The Affordable Care Act at least addresses this issue by insisting citizens have coverage or pay a fine. For those states that enrolled, there is help for the poor, but almost as many states have opted out of the Federal system. How do Americans in those states afford health care? A single payer system like Medicare for all would provide coverage for everyone and make sure that premiums were affordable. Health care is a clear example of, "We all do better when we all do better."

Public health experts advocate enhancing preventive care by instilling healthy behaviors in us all. To accomplish this worthy goal, we need to make sure that people are more aware of taking care of their health and aim public education efforts at encouraging them to do so. I believe that with a comprehensive single-payer system, public education measures would be easier to institute. A universal system would have another advantage that I'm sure all of us would welcome—our coverage would be stable and we could stay with our chosen providers. Flux governs the present system. Changing jobs or seeking more affordable care often means changing plans and providers. This, in turn, forces us to learn new rules, find new doctors, and leave our familiar clinics and hospitals. Under a single-insurer plan, changes would be made by the patient, not the insurer.

Beyond the Affordable Care Act: An Economic Analysis of a Unified System of Health Care for Minnesota, a report prepared by Amy Lang for Growth & Justice, analyzed where we are and where we could be if we had a unified and universal system for Minnesota. A principal finding of the study is that "Total state health spending can be reduced by nearly 9% under a unified single-payer plan while eliminating uninsurance in the state. The savings are achieved despite covering the remaining 262,000 Minnesotans who would still be uninsured under the Affordable Care Act. Minnesota families, most employers, and taxpayers would all benefit from a unified system." According to the report, there was one downside. Minnesota could lose 42,000 jobs in health care administration if we went to a single-payer system. I was happy to read that those jobs would largely be made up by employment growth in other sectors of the economy. What really caught my attention, however, is that we have 42,000 *extra* jobs for people doing paperwork for private insurers! Remember that the next time you here someone is singing a song about how efficient our current system is. In Minnesota, insurance companies just announced rate increases to feed the bloated system. Here is the Governor's response to health insurance rate increases in Minnesota's private individual market, "I am extremely unhappy with these extremely high insurance rate increases. The insurance companies, who are responsible for them, will force Minnesotans into plans with less complete coverage or drive them out of the insurance market entirely. Given these large rate increases, I strongly encourage Minnesotans to shop on MNsure so they can access tax credits to help reduce their costs. If health insurance companies make good coverage unaffordable for Americans, I believe citizens will soon demand that insurers' excessive administrative overheads be eliminated, and that they be removed as the providers of health insurance."

Excessive cost is only one of many disadvantages of our multi-provider private system. Citizens have fewer good choices and options for health care than they would under a single payer system. Market incentives built into the health system discourage citizens from taking care of their health needs and make them less likely to seek help early on. We need a health system that delivers what citizens want and deserve. We need a system that assures people they can get guidance and care from the health care providers they want. Government has a role to play in making this happen. Instead, budget cut talk dominates care discussions and policy makers call for repeal of existing reforms rather than implementaion of new ones. Medicare and Medicaid seem headed for cuts, not expansion. This is serious business, literally life and death. A study by Harvard Medical School linked lack of health care coverage to about 45,000 deaths a year in the United States. People without health insurance face risk of death at a 40 percent higher rate than individuals with private health insurance. The uninsured die because the public hospitals they rely on are closing or cutting back services. To make matters worse, for the most part improvements in treating chronic conditions like high blood pressure benefit only those with insurance.

In March 2013, the Minnesota State Legislature created MNsure, Minnesota's state-based health insurance exchange mandated under the Affordable Care Act. MNsure, while an imperfect system, is the largest expansion of health care in generations. A report from the University of Minnesota's State Health Access Data Assistance Center published in June 2014 found that MNsure cut the number of uninsured Minnesotans nearly in half. "A change in the un-insurance rate like this is pretty much unprecedented in Minnesota," said Julie Sonier, co-author of the report. Minnesotans will no longer have to pay for the uncompensated care of their neighbors who previously lacked insurance and, by necessity, sought care through the emergency room system. As of the end of MNsure's first open enrollment period, 95% of Minnesotans have health insurance. This is the second highest insured rate in the entire country. We included common sense consumer protections that prevented insurers from charging women higher premiums than men or denying care to people with pre-existing conditions. We also eliminated limits on the amount of care you can receive in a year or your lifetime. By expanding access to affordable health care, MNsure is also helping to address significant, persistent health disparities among our citizens of color. For example, African American and Latino women are more likely to be diagnosed with later-stage breast cancer due to their lack of health care access under our previous system.

In spite of the progress we have made, much work remains to be done. Our health care system continues to offer so much less than we should expect in a wealthy country. As Trudy Lieberman wrote in *Harper's Magazine*, "And what of those middle-class Americans who were supposed to benefit from the law, and were promised that they could keep the policies and health providers they already had? They've already been hit with higher premiums and higher out-of pocket costs—and people with top of-the-line coverage from their employers will soon find those policies shrinking, thanks to a provision of the law that encourages companies to offer less-generous benefits . . . accelerating the Great Cost Shift, which transfers the growing price of medical care to patients themselves through high deductibles, coinsurance, copayments, and limited provider networks (which sometimes offer so little choice that patients end up seeking out-of-network care and paying on their own)."

Many of my constituents who contact me lately about MNSure are concerned that we are still making access to health care more difficult with extra charges, copays, and high deductibles. Clearly there is more work to be done. As we move forward, let us remember that Japan and many European countries provide better health care to their citizens than we do in the United States. Those countries also have more equal income distributions than we do. In short, the more a country supports a middle class economy, the more likely it will have universal, affordable health care. The widening income gap in our country affects us in many ways, none of them good, but none as serious as the health care crisis we now face. We can do better with our health care system, but only if we do better with our economy. Piecemeal solutions in the United States have failed and will continue to do so. We need a comprehensive approach, one that both restores our middle class society and, as part of the bargain, gives us the health care system we deserve.

American lives are at stake.

Foundations:

TRANSPORTATION

Potholes in the Road to Prosperity

"Every $1 billion invested in public transportation capital/operations creates or supports: 36,000 jobs, $3.6 billion in business sales, and nearly $500 million in federal, state, and local tax revenues."
—Economic Development Research Group

A township supervisor in my legislative district called me after an important state transportation bill failed to pass in 2007. "Do you know if the bridge on 140th Street is going to be repaired?" he asked. "You should take a drive by sometime and have a look at it." I did just that and, deeply concerned by what I saw, contacted our county transportation engineer. He told me that funding was tight and that repairs on the bridge would have to wait a few years. Upon receiving the disappointing news, the township supervisor said, "I hope that bridge can hold. God forbid somebody should be on that bridge when it fails." He knew neighbors would continue to cross the bridge every day. Two days later, the I-35W bridge in downtown Minneapolis collapsed into the Mississippi River during rush hour. Thirteen people died, another 130 were injured, and countless more around the country worried if any loved ones were on the bridge when it went down.

There could be no more dramatic a reminder of how badly

we have neglected our transportation system than what happened in Minneapolis. As attention turned to the question of what other bridges across the country needed attention, a frightening answer came back—we learned from the Federal Highway Administration that Americans were driving on 130,646 bridges (almost one in four of all the nation's bridges) that were judged "deficient," either by deterioration or by their obsolete designs. As the replacement bridge was being built in Minneapolis, retired Army General Barry R. McCaffrey wrote, "While safety rightly has been the central concern of Minnesotans following last year's collapse, the threat of inadequate infrastructure not only places citizens at risk, it threatens the economic vitality of the state." Calling our transportation problems "as serious as a heart attack," he went on to say that, as a percentage of gross domestic product, our nation now spends less than half as much on infrastructure as it did in the 1960's.

The lesson from the bridge collapse was further impressed upon me during an Energy Committee hearing I attended in the Minnesota State Legislature. We heard from Matthew R. Simmons, an energy investment banker from Houston, Texas, and author of the best-selling book *Twilight in the Desert*. Both the book and his testimony were primarily about the declining future of Saudi Oil, and what we must do about it. Mr. Simmons made many thoughtful points and told us that that 60 to 70 percent of the world's oil is used in transportation and over 95 percent of transportation fuel is oil. As the hearing was concluding, Mr. Simmons said he had one more thing to say: "But a far greater and immediate danger than Peak Oil we face here in the U.S. is the sorry state of our rusting infrastructure, you could call it 'peak rust.' If we don't do something about it our bridges will be falling and our buildings will crumble without even having to fly planes into them." It was a chilling comment, missed by most in the meeting as the press and legislators packed up to leave.

I had a similar experience in 2015 at a hearing before the Legislative Water Commission where testifiers described the hopless condition of the nation's pipelines. It was yet another example of how neglect is taking its toll on America's infrastructure. In 2008, CNN reported that our nation's bridges were in such poor shape that it would cost at least $140 billion to repair them if we started right away. If we delayed, costs would only go up. The article cited a nationwide comprehensive safety report titled "Bridging the Gap" that spelled things out in frightening detail. Almost three-fourths of US road traffic and 90 percent of truck traffic travel over state-owned bridges. According to the report, one in four of those bridges is in need of repair. The average age of America's bridges is 43, only seven years shy of the maximum age for which most were designed. One in five US bridges is more than 50 years old.

Since then, we have seen a great deal of political rhetoric, almost all of it unsupported by meaningful action. Consider these three bullet points from Minnesota Governor Mark Dayton's 2015 plan for Minnesota's transportation system:

- Right now, more than half of Minnesota's roads are more than 50 years old, and 40 percent of the state's bridges are more than 40 years old. In just the next three years alone, one in five Minnesota roads will pass their useful life. And in the next ten years, nearly 40 percent of our roads will be past their useful life.

- Poor roads cost Minnesota motorists $1.2 billion every year in extra vehicle repairs, and Minnesota businesses spend an extra $232 million each year on additional freight transportation costs caused by traffic congestion.

- The average Minnesota commuter wastes 34 hours stuck in traffic every year. If no additional investments are made in our transportation systems, by 2025 the average Minnesota commuter will waste an estimated 45 hours stuck in traffic.

As you can see, there has been precious little done since the 35W bridge collapse, and much more remains to be done. Yet all across the nation, even from politicians living in states in which there is a constitutional commitment to assure well-maintained transportation, we hear the time-old objection that we can't afford what must be done. In their zeal for cutting taxes, too many of them forget that paying for roads and public transportation is crucial to economic growth. Here in Minnesota, barely a year after the bridge collapse had transportation front and center in everyone's mind, then-Governor Pawlenty vetoed a transportation bill that included a gas tax increase. Fortunately, we had enough votes to override him and pass the first increase in the Minnesota gas tax in 20 years. Meanwhile, other state governors put ideology above the needs of their state by refusing to accept federal funds for high-speed rail.

Minnesota has a history of pay-as-you-go transportation funding so future generations do not have to pay for roads we travel on today. The gas tax is a pure user fee that is constitutionally dedicated to roads and bridges (it cannot be used for transit), so it is generally the first place we look for additional long-term road repair dollars. The other two main transportation funding sources—again, user-fee based—are tab fees and the motor vehicle sales tax. Less significant sources include federal aid, the motor vehicle sales lease tax, bonds, and smaller sources such as construction work performed under an agreement with local units of government, fees for permits, and fines. If we were to look elsewhere for transportation dollars, one option would be from the general fund. The downside is that this would then set up a competition with other essential services like education, health care, and public safety. Other funding suggestions have been floated at the Capitol, including a surcharge on hybrid vehicles, a mileage tax, and toll roads. For various reasons, all these suggestions have their supporters and detractors.

North Dakota has a state-owned bank, which is able to finance various projects, and the United States once had the Reconstruction Finance Corporation (RFC) to facilitate economic activity by lending money during the Great Depression. It financed the construction and operation of war plants, made loans to foreign governments, provided protection against war and disaster damages, provided financial support to state and local governments, and made loans to banks, railroads, mortgage associations, and other businesses. Its aim was to boost the country's confidence and help banks return to performing daily functions during the Depression. It continued to operate through the New Deal, where it became more prominent, and throughout World War II. Between the time it was created in 1932 and the time it was disbanded in 1957, the RFC made loans of approximately $50 billion. Perhaps a public bank at the state or national level could be used for infrastructure. State-owned banks generate revenue without raising taxes and offer affordable alternatives for public infrastructure projects at lower borrowing costs. Creating such an alternative, however, would be politically challenging even though in our current impasse it could make a lot of sense.

Government has a role to play in providing basic transportation infrastructure. It is another of those "we" investments that even economics texts say cannot, and should not, be provided solely by the market system. We have recognized this for our entire history as a nation. Way back, during the 1870's to the 1920's, a major political force called the Good Roads Movement sought increased government funding of and involvement in building roads and highways by turning local agitation into a national political campaign. Roads in those days were dirt or gravel: muddy in the winter and dusty in the summer. Early organizers cited Europe where road construction and maintenance were supported by national and local governments. The main goal of the movement was to help rural populations gain the social and economic benefits enjoyed by cities, where citizens benefited from railroads, trolleys, and paved streets. Even more than traditional horse-drawn vehicles, the newly-invented bicycle could benefit from good country roads.

The rapid rise in automobile ownership and use after 1907–09 propelled the Good Roads Movement to success. From 1900 to 1907 a total of 154,000 motor vehicles were produced in the United States. Production continued to climb to 895,000 in 1915 and 1.525 million in 1916. It became clear that the country needed a national road system. It was no longer enough to get states, counties, cities, and towns to build roads. A system was needed that set standards for road design, road signage, and ensured that major population centers were linked. The National Highways Association adopted the slogan "Good Roads Everywhere" and quickly raised funds to publish a map of a proposed 50,000-mile National Highways network. Founder and President Charles

Henry Davis spoke of "a broad and comprehensive system of National Highways, built, owned, and maintained by the National Government. Only the nation can build the roads heavy enough, wide enough, straight enough for our national industrial and military needs." On July 11, 1916, President Woodrow Wilson signed the Federal Aid Road Act of 1916 into law. This was the first federal highway funding legislation in the United States, and it fulfilled one of the planks in the platform on which Wilson had run: the happiness, comfort, and prosperity of rural life, and the development of the city alike are conserved by the construction of public highways.

Small government can't do big transportation projects. We had to wait for the New Deal and the Second World War for government to become big enough to provide us with the bridges, roads, and interchanges that were beyond the means of for-profit corporations to undertake. We set to work on creating the Interstate Highway System that brought us all closer together and opened countless new business opportunities. Those days appear to be behind us. We seem content to watch our wonders of the world rust and degrade. Jeff Madrick in *The Case for Big Government* says, "When the American Society of Civil Engineers gives American infrastructure—including highways, airports, and water facilities—an average grade of D, it is simply difficult to respond." It is, he says, "a failure to recognize change."

Bob Herbert quotes the 2013 report card of the American Society of Engineers, "The health of our nation's bridges is directly tied to the nation's ability to compete in a global market . . . Approximately 210 million trips are taken daily across deficient bridges in the nation's 102 largest metropolitan regions." He then explains that it isn't only bridges that are the problem and provides the following list:

"Badly congested roads and highways that are often in such disrepair that they are hazards to human life and a drag on economic activity.

"Wasteful, overburdened, and increasingly decrepit water and sewer systems that date back in some cases to the late nineteenth and early twentieth centuries.

"Aging, fragile, and poorly maintained dams and levees (think New Orleans) that are a perennial threat to public safety.

"A haphazard and often unreliable system of electrical power so hobbled by poor maintenance and excessive demand that it will require more than $1 trillion to bring it up to twenty first century standards by 2030.

"An outdated air traffic control system that keeps passengers bogged down with costly and nerve racking delays and that has experienced many harrowing near misses."

Transportation, especially personal transportation, is often the underpinning of an individual's economic security. Available and affordable transportation dictates the jobs one can accept, the education and training one can pursue, and the care one can provide for children and aging parents. This is as true in rural areas as it is in our cities. Pia Lopez wrote an excellent article on the special transportation needs of our rural areas in the *St. Paul Legal Ledger Capitol Report*. The rural areas of Minnesota, like those of most of the United States, have an aging population that is less likely to choose individual automobiles as their primary means of transportation. Often the cars they can afford are unreliable and need constant repairs. Single, working women desperately need transportation options since their choices are often complicated when dependent children are involved. Efforts to teach women about making routine maintenance to their cars helps but doesn't address the need for a dependable transportation system in rural areas. A Millennial living in rural Minnesota often does not have the money, or even the desire their parents had, to own a car. Poverty rates in rural areas can be shockingly high, providing still another reason for Lopez to conclude that we need a transportation-funding package that "does much more than maintain roads and highways in rural Minnesota." The way we design and build transportation options for using those roads and bridges is also critical.

Minnesota, like other states, is grappling with how to build a sustainable, efficient, high quality, safe transportation system that allows businesses to transport goods and services, people to get to and from their jobs, and consumers to travel in their communities to take advantage of recreation, entertainment and other activities. Despite the ongoing and stubborn opposition to truly addressing our state's transportation needs, whether roads, bridges, highways, intercity rail, or public transportation, the Minnesota State Legislature has taken several steps in the right direction. The $5.2 billion transportation bill that was passed in 2013 included $1.7 billion for state road construction and a $300 million "down payment" on Minnesota's Corridors of Commerce program that will fund critical safety and mobility improvements along key trunk highway routes in rural areas. In addition to the transportation budget, the legislature passed a bonding bill that included over $100 million for roads, bridges and transit. This is a start, but only a start. As I write this, Governor Dayton is seeking six billion over the next ten years to get us where we need to be.

A good friend of mine is an economist. He, like all economists

I know, tends to be cynical at times. When I told him our Governor was seeking $6 billion to get Minnesota's transportation system back into the shape it needs to be in, he quipped, "Wow! How many tax cuts will it take to raise that kind of money?" Then, in a more serious mood, he reminded me of a business concept called "living off depreciation." Generations before us built and paid for a world-class transportation system that supported a middle class economy. But, more recently, legislatures chose tax cuts over maintaining and improving that system. Instead of building roads and bridges, we built an economy with a Third World income distribution. That strategy has now run its course. We have a lot of making up to do for our shortsighted decisions of the past few decades.

Our middle class economy requires a safe and reliable transportation system. We must address the transportation needs of our people and our economy. Workers need to get to work in a safe and timely manner. Businesses need cost-efficient, reliable ways to move products from place to place. When we do the right thing for our transportation system, we do the right thing for all of us, not just the handful at the top. These basic principles should guide legislative and policy decisions. Instead, we see legislative gridlock, calls to cut budgets, and an excessive focus on protecting the interests of corporations. Meanwhile, our transportation system falls deeper and deeper into disrepair. Here, as with other aspects of our middle class economy, turning things around will take more, much more, than any single piece of legislation can hope to provide. It will take a comprehensive approach that puts rebuilding our middle class economy front and center.

Foundations:

ENERGY SYSTEMS THAT MAINTAIN A CLEAN AND SAFE ENVIRONMENT

A Rising Tide Will Sink All Boats

Energy conservation, mass transit, and renewable energy development all hold great promise in moving us to a cleaner, safer world. In addition, they provide potential for significant economic development and job creation. We all have dreams of what our lives will be, and even more of what we want for our children and grandchildren. Many of those dreams will become real only if we have the right policies concerning energy and its use. Here, as in so many other areas, what politicians say and what they do can be hard to reconcile. Corporate cash speaks louder than scientists and citizens.

In his book *How the Economy Was Lost,* Paul Craig Roberts worries that an unregulated market economy will continue on its path toward the destruction of life on earth. Externalities are not very important in "an empty world," he says, but in a "full world" ignored externalities can offset the value of increased output. "Externalities" are what economists call those costs to society caused by pollution. They result in private profits and social costs for all of us. Since the costs are borne by society in general, and not solely by the individual responsible, economists call externalities "market failures." That's right—failures of the market system to guide us on the right path. The case for government intervention couldn't be clearer; instead, we get calls from corporations and the politicians they support to "cut regulations." Again, to quote Paul Craig Roberts, the cost of relying on markets alone is frightening, indeed: "If the future is left to take care of itself, organized society in the U.S. could fail. . . . To conclude that our future is a continuation of the past is a death warrant for U.S. society."

We must also recognize the link between jobs and policy on a global scale. Globalization has allowed multi-national corporations to tear down our own manufacturing capability and rebuild it in foreign countries. It will be very difficult, and maybe impossible, to reacquire the manufacturing capability we have given away. Over a century ago, Thorstein Veblen recognized that once we lost the skills and knowledge learned through this kind of work it would be nearly impossible to bring them back. Globalization promised more jobs, cheaper goods, and worldwide prosperity, but instead we have students graduating from our universities who can only find work as waitresses, bartenders, and cab drivers. Our trade deficit threatens the stability of our entire economy. How could things go so wrong? Of course, other countries offer lower wages and weaker labor standards, and that is part of the problem. But it is not the entire problem. The Third World destinations of our manufacturing jobs have virtually no environmental regulations, so we, in a way, export pollution without regard to the old saying that "what goes around comes around." At the same time, our refusal to develop sustainable energy sources leaves us economically and politically beholden to foreign energy suppliers.

It's very difficult to address these issues head-on. Writing in the *Atlantic Monthly*, Julio Friedman examined "Why it is hard to talk about energy." He said, "America created the energy system it wanted—cheap, unobtrusive and all but invisible." Many of us never see oil wells, refineries, power plants, substations, natural gas pipelines, oil trains, or storage facilities. Most people don't know how much energy they use. There is a disconnect between the value of that energy, whether it's electricity or gasoline, and the actual cost. The value of energy for each person is much higher than what they pay for it. How many of us could survive without it? Difficult or not, energy policy is something we must discuss. We cannot continue to rely so heavily on corporations and their lobbyists.

In what I consider the absolute low point of United States energy policy, Vice President Cheney, former CEO of Haliburton, met behind closed doors with the country's dominant energy producers during the early years of the George W. Bush administration. He wouldn't say who was in the room, much less what was discussed. One can only speculate on what deals were made and how little attention was paid to the interests of people like you and me as that roomful of tycoons set our energy policies.

In his article "The Real American Exceptionalism," David Morris provides another thoughtful perspective on why we have not been able to be better stewards of our natural resources. Many political leaders believe the term "American exceptionalism" means that we are "inherently superior to the world's other nations." Morris offers a different view: our "exceptionalism'" has come from the "exceptionally favorable circumstances the United States found itself in at its founding and over its first 200 years." He finds us also exceptional in the way that we have squandered those advantages. Morris argues that, because of our abundant resources, we could afford a value system based almost exclusively on rugged individualism and personal liberty. Now that our natural resources are no longer abundant, more appropriate values of working together and embracing new systems of cooperation and mutual benefit are needed. We have largely lost the concept of common good, or, perhaps, never had it to begin with. Put another way, Americans have put too much emphasis on skill, hard work, and market systems, and not enough emphasis on luck and the grace of God in explaining our rise to global prominence.

As difficult as the task before us appears, we must move forward aggressively if we want to salvage our grandchildren's future. Here again, David Morris provides useful guidance. He advises us to think of systems that are not so centralized and, therefore, invisible to most of us. In books like *Self-Reliant Cities* and *Seeing the Light*, he writes about the need to democratize and distribute our energy production. In his view, advances in technology and the rapid pace of resource depletion have made it possible for individual citizens to produce their own energy with solar panels and wind turbines. This idea is not as far-fetched as it may at first sound. Consider the "feed-in tariff" approach used in Germany and other countries. The policy works by insisting that utilities purchase energy from individuals at a premium price. Citizen investment in energy production becomes affordable and stimulates a growing solar and wind industry. The result has been an economic transformation that has generated 450,000 "green" jobs. Today, Germany is a world leader in renewable energy with more solar collectors than any country in the world. The German economy benefits by about $9 billion per year through new jobs, lower energy costs, and reduced energy dependence on other countries.

Contrast the German experience with our own. According to the Energy Information Agency, our federal energy trade deficit is approximately $1 billion a day, or more than $10,000 a second. To fuel our economy we depend on unstable and unfriendly nations who don't share American values. Our most respected military leaders recognize that climate change is a threat multiplier for instability in the most volatile regions of the world. Our centralized system puts us all at increasing risk of failure. To quote former CIA Director R. James Woolsey, "At peak periods, our current electricity grid is overburdened and fragile and relies on a small number of gigantic (often highly polluting) power plants." Woolsey also talked about a feed-in tariff policy implemented by Gainesville, Florida, as a solution to this problem. Moving toward electricity produced by renewable sources distributed across a grid would result in far better security, resilience, and sustainability.

Developing new, decentralized energy sources is one side of a coin; the other is conserving energy, no matter the source. Willy Vogt, one of the German legislators responsible for establishing feed-in tariff policy, says the least expensive and most efficient power plant is the one you don't have to build because you have a policy to make more energy available by reducing demand. Thus, German energy policies encourage people to weatherize homes and use appliances and equipment that are more energy efficient. Both businesses and homeowners are encouraged to evaluate their energy use with meters. Energy users turn off lights and equipment when not in use and install more energy-efficient light bulbs and other equipment. Following this lead, American legislators and policy makers, even some utilities, have developed similar policies to inform consumers how they can conserve energy. Some of the stimulus money put in place by the Obama administration went to weatherization projects. In addition, policy makers struggle with how to pay for energy differently so that utilities are not threatened by declining levels of consumption and profits while still allowing consumers to see savings from reduced energy use. This is an area where labor unions and environmentalists have formed a coalition, the Blue Green Alliance, to find ways to create good jobs with the environment in mind. Leading the way in state policy, the State of Hawaii has just made a commitment to achieve 100% energy production from renewables by 2045.

Developing a 21st century mass transportation system must be part of our energy planning. More transit options will give people viable choices for reducing energy use and saving money. Formerly, cheap gas, low-cost electricity, and open land near cities led us to build interstate highways and massive suburbs. Today, expensive energy, high levels of pollution, and longer and longer commutes in order to find affordable housing demand a new direction for our policies. We've also learned that cutting up our communities with roads and freeways because of a car-dependent culture has hurt both communities and community development. City planners now realize they must incorporate new ideas that blend energy use, transportation design, and use of public space in ways that rebuild our sense of community. Planning of this kind should also include affordable housing and the particular needs of rural population centers. The lack of affordable housing forces the poor to look for housing in small communities where cars are the only transportation option. In many cases poor rural residents can't afford reliable cars nor the fuel to power them. Even though housing may be affordable, they have no reasonable way to get to work and sustain their income.

The United States has only five percent of the world's population, but consumes 25 percent of the world's oil. At this writing, 55 percent of our oil is imported; by 2020 that number could grow to 65 percent. The way to prevent such dangerous reliance, we are told, is to ignore the obvious environmental issues associated with shale oil exploitation. With an overburdened and terrorist-threatened airline industry, we need to explore high-speed rail to connect the great expanse of our country. At the same time, city and urban planners must think about more compact urban areas with more efficient use of energy. Buses and commuter rail can reduce congestion, pollution, and commuting times. We have a situation where issues come together: 90 percent of our citizens on public assistance do not have cars. Without adequate alternatives, their opportunities for work and fuller lives disappear.

By any public measure, mass transit is a great investment. But that investment will not happen if we continue to entrust our future to politicians fronting for a well-funded and well-organized fossil fuel industry. If we look at our policy history for the past several decades, we see glimmers of hope and clouds of despair. After the fuel crisis of the 1970's, President Carter formed the Energy Department and began moving us toward development of renewable and synthetic fuels. Other difficulties his presidency faced forced him out of office and the opportunity was lost. President Reagan oversaw a reversal of all renewable energy gains, thus assuring we would remain dependent on fossil fuel energy. By the beginning of this century, the concept of a democratically-determined, sensible energy policy had been thrown out the window. Had the American economy in the 1970s been encouraged and turned loose on developing home-grown renewable energy for energy independence, we would not have been held hostage by OPEC and might have avoided extensive involvement in wars in the Middle East. Instead we would have a manufacturing economy selling turbines and solar panels all over the world. We would be well on our way to solving the global warming problem and have a much cleaner environment overall. We would not be struggling to fill gas-guzzling vehicles with expensive gasoline while oil companies posted record profits. We would not face trillions of dollars of debt because of unfunded wars.

Why haven't we taken the sensible path toward sustainability and prosperity, rather than one leading to the brink of disaster? Much of the answer lies in the way we have focused only on "me" at the expense of "we." We have perverted Senator Wellstone's words to "We all do better when the top one percent does better" and hear empty phrases like "a rising tide floats all boats." When David Cay Johnston asked high school students, "What is the purpose of the United States?," they replied, "To make people rich." Johnston thinks the way those students responded should not surprise us in light of the reshaping of government's relationship with private interests, which he describes as "a vision of lower taxes, less regulation, and maximum economic leeway for those at the top . . . the pursuit of wealth is the warp and weft of America; everything else will follow." Johnston's response to this blind view is that the preamble to the Constitution succinctly tells us our nation's purpose in six principles: society, justice, peace, security, commonwealth, and freedom. Someone's individual ability to become excessively rich is not one of them. Riches are a product of the society that created our nation, not the reason it exists. There is no "me" in many of the most important issues we face relating to energy and the environment. We all share the same climate, breathe the same air, depend on the same sources of water, and waste the same petroleum reserves. There is, therefore, no way that a philosophy of me, and only me, can guide us in a time of scarcity and crisis. The past several decades have led us not to a brighter, more democratic energy policy, but to a closed-door meeting of energy giants. The way forward must emerge from the best of the values we find in the concept of the common good.

In 2014, the challenges facing our planet in terms of climate change and sustainable energy were on full display in Minnesota. Exceedingly harsh and unpredictable cold winter weather was made worse by a significant propane shortage that brought outrageously high prices and fear of running out altogether for some rural communities. A few months later, more than half of Minnesota's counties had fallen under state and federal disaster declarations in the aftermath of torrential rain and heavy flooding. As incredible as it seems to me, energy lobbyists and conservative think tanks still deny climate change and encourage a "go slow" attitude that benefits energy companies at the expense of everyone else. Sure, there is risk in moving too fast. But, as the report *Action Without Regrets in a Climate of Uncertainty: Smart Investments with Immediate Benefits* reminds us, the risks of doing nothing are sometimes greater:

> *That the climate of Minnesota and the world is changing is clear. While it also is true that there is no consensus on precisely how fast change will occur and precisely how much change there will be, decision-makers must recognize that to be prudent risk managers they must take intelligent risks today.*
>
> *If decision-makers choose to avoid risk completely because we cannot define with precision how much and how fast change will occur or there is no complete public consensus, they risk significant impacts on core Minnesota industries; disruptions in transportation of goods and materials, as the Mississippi River faces both low flows from drought*

and unmanageable flows from floods; changes in ecosystems, including damage to the state's sport fishing and hunting industries; and threats to public health. If decision-makers respond effectively—that is, take intelligent risks—they will set the table for a stable economy and to protect public health.

Embracing the concepts of risk management provides a way of making the required decisions. Identifying smart investments in actions we won't regret is a wise choice for a sustainable future. This is not being a daredevil. It is being a wise steward of Minnesota's future.

Although there is little that a single state can do to solve the global climate problem, we must not throw up our hands in despair. Minnesota is leading among states when it comes to providing sustainable energy, reducing pollution and cutting down on carbon emissions that science tells us are responsible for climate change. State lawmakers provided the same kick-start to solar power that the wind industry received 20 years ago by establishing a 1.5 percent solar energy production requirement by 2020 (and a stated goal of 10 percent by 2030) as well as incentives to encourage the development of solar resources. Here is one area where thoughtful, responsible action by each state can make a significant difference in leading federal policy away from the lobbyists that now control it. I encourage leaders in every state to develop other initiatives that, together, will put us back on the right track of sensible energy use and production all across our economy.

In their book, *Cradle to Cradle,* architects William McDonough and Michael Braungart said:

Consider this: all the ants on the planet, taken to-gether, have a biomass greater than that of humans. Ants have been incredibly industrious for millions of years. Yet their productiveness nourishes plants, ani-mals and soil. Human industry has been in full swing for little over a century, yet it has brought about a de-cline in almost every ecosystem on the planet. Nature doesn't have a design problem. People do.

Working together to build clean, sustainable energy and food systems that are regenerative rather than destructive is some-thing we must do if our grandchildren are to have any hope of growing up in a middle class society. The alternative is skyrock-eting energy prices, an unstable climate, and rising sea levels that sink, not float, all boats.

Foundations:

L I V I N G   W A G E S

Working More, Making Less

In his book *Take This Job and Ship It*, former North Dakota Senator Byron Dorgan begins with a story about a workingman who was standing in line to pay his last respects to President Franklin D. Roosevelt. "'Did you know the President?" a reporter asked him. "No," the man said through tears, "but he knew me." Dorgan goes on to ask, "Who is seeing the working man today?" Most of us sit by helplessly as corporation after corporation ships middle class jobs to third world countries. Politicians across the country invariably come upon out-of-work industrial workers who ask them what they can do about the wholesale sell-off of jobs in America. All too often, the politician has no response and no idea what to do. Worse yet, some extreme free-market ideologues might say that what is happening to so many American workers is actually a good thing, something that in the long run will make our economy better off. Of course, most of those making such claims have high-paying, stable jobs representing the interests of the financial elite.

The last thirty years have seen a corporate war against the American worker. That war now extends into political campaigns highlighting global competitiveness, an assault on labor unions, and a relentless push for most of us to work more for less. Those politicians are supported by the very corporations that have sent our jobs overseas when they could and imported cheap labor when they couldn't. In the 1990's alone, according to Greg Palast, multinational companies let go 2.9 million workers in America. At the same time, their foreign workforces increased by 2.7 million. This war, waged on multiple fronts from the boardroom to the courtroom and all levels of government, has resulted in an ever-shrinking supply of jobs that pay enough to support a middle class way of life.

The result of this economic war on working people was starkly portrayed by the *StarTribune* in a front page story with a title that pretty much says it all: "Workers' Aspirations Stagnate with Pay." Three sad and worried faces of some of my fellow Minnesotans told the story. One, a 36-year-old warehouse worker with twenty years of experience, said, "It's a job, but I feel I'm worth more than $10.75 an hour." Another, a 59-year old truck driver, told how he could live well on the 41-cents-a-mile he made sixteen years ago, but now he was making the exact same amount in the face of much higher living costs. He works six days a week instead of the five he used to and still can barely make ends meet. He said, "Everybody that I know, no one's getting a raise." The third, a 44-year-old attorney, could not find well-paying work ten years ago. She borrowed heavily to earn an MBA degree, only to find herself $250,000 in debt and working temporary jobs reviewing legal documents. Pay for such work has dropped from $26 per hour five years ago to $22 per hour today.

These are by no means isolated cases. Economist Robert Reich wrote this about the battered American middle class: "Having been roughed up, they face years of catch-up to get to where they once were. They feel poorer because they are poorer. They feel less secure because they are less secure. The crisis's severity—and the fact that it surprised most 'experts'—shocked them. The large income and wealth losses compounded their sense of vulnerability." Vulnerability. That's a good way to put it. Wages for new hires, adjusted for inflation, have been heading downward since 2006 in Minnesota and fell to $11.64 in 2011. The minimum wage went from one of the lowest in the country to $9.50. A family of three (the average family size in Minnesota) would need an hourly wage of $16.34 to make it. How can anyone feel secure and support a family with that kind of discrepancy?

One of our state's labor market economists commented on how, even with a low 3.2 percent rate of unemployment, wages aren't picking up. He said, "Everyone from the Federal Reserve to labor market information directors are wondering when wage growth is going to start to appear." That same question has bothered me for a long time now. The conclusion I am coming to is, "Never. At least not as long as we keep doing what we are doing." People working full-time deserve the dignity of a living wage, but our policies are moving us in the opposite direction.

While some corporations work to reduce wages directly, others pressure local governments into deals that lower their contribution toward taxes. This, too, weakens our middle class economy. In *A Governor's Story*, Jennifer Granholm of Michigan described her harrowing struggle to fight for jobs and America's middle class economy. She tried everything from tax cuts to incentives in an attempt to keep companies from leaving and to attract new ones to Michigan. She was at the center of the economic downturn in Detroit where unemployment reached depression era levels. Unfortunately for Michigan, term limits ended her role as governor. Granholm was forced to watch as outsiders bankrolled a new administration and the undoing of her good work. Her experience taught her the futility of states allowing themselves to be played against each other. Rather, states should work together with the federal government. Only at that level can government effectively step in and work with the private sector to accelerate recovery. As she said, "Hands-off, laissez-faire, free market economics will only ensure that other governments step into the void. America can either take action on behalf of its citizens or watch passively as our people and businesses lose to more determined foreign competitors."

While Governor Granholm saw danger in determined efforts of committed foreign competitors, George Packer saw another sinister force at work. In his article "The Broken Contract" he described how in 1978 American life changed dramatically. It was a time, in his words, "of widespread pessimism–high inflation, high unemployment, high gas prices." It was also a time when "the country reacted to its sense of decline by moving away from the social arrangement that had been in place since the 1930's and 40's." He described what Nobel-Prize winning economist Paul Samuelson called a "mixed economy" and refers to it as "a middle class democracy" supported by an "unwritten social contract." That contract among labor, business, and government included everyone, not only the wealthy elite. The benefits of the economic boom at the end of World War II would, under the contract, be distributed widely across all groups. Government policies and laws sought to maintain a healthy balance between workers' wages and corporate profits. As a result, widespread gains in purchasing power fueled growth by increasing demand for goods and services across the board. Progressive tax policies restricted the amount of wealth that could accumulate at the very top and prevented the "inherited plutocracy" that arises when estate taxes are out of balance. This contract was still in play up through the 1970's, when corporate executives earned

40 times as much as their lowest-paid employees. By 2014, that same salary ratio had ballooned to 600 to 1.

A middle class economy is about balance. If those who create jobs get too small a share, they have no incentive to do what they must do and the economy breaks down. On the other hand, if those who work for a living don't make a living wage, they don't have the purchasing power to fuel economic growth. Where are we now? In July 2011, *The Wall Street Journal* featured a story with a title that answers that question: "Corporate profits share of pie most in 60 years." The article said, among other things, that "the fat cats are fatter than we thought, and the incomes of regular folk are worse than we thought." We tilt too much toward those who own corporations and are supposed to create jobs, and we lean too far from the wages needed to maintain a growing economy. It turns out the imbalance pointed out in the *Journal* article has not always existed. The years between 1958 and 1977 never saw the share of national income going to the top one percent rise above 11.2 percent. By 1988, the share going to the top one percent had increased to 15.5 percent. During the next twenty years, that share increased steadily and in 2007 reached 23.5 percent, a level not seen since the beginning of the Great Depression. Since then, we have been stuck at Depression-era income distribution levels.

What can we do? First, we must recognize that our out-of-balance income distribution results from falling wages and unemployment, not from a pie that is too small. The United States economy is still the largest in the world, so there should be enough to go around. Instead, we find that another *Wall Street Journal* article reported: "wages and salaries account for the smallest share of GDP since 1955. . . . Fewer people are working and the ones who are working aren't getting raises." Many other studies confirm what many already suspect: wages haven't kept up with inflation for the past few decades. The gradual suffocation of our middle class economy has been going on for a long time.

Once we have seen that the problem is an imbalance of wages and corporate profits, we can move on to what we can do to get wages back to where they need to be. There are three primary policy areas that either have favored or harmed our middle class economy: tax policy, trade policy, and labor policy. Let's take them one at a time and see where we are going, and how we can do better.

If we're to address our income distribution problem and rebuild our middle class economy, we must have higher taxes on the very wealthy. Instead, we are heading in the opposite direction. Our federal income tax system protects the super rich on an increasingly grand scale. The current maximum federal income tax rate is 39 percent. Most of the very rich pay a lower rate on much of their income. Stock dividends are treated as capital gains and are, therefore, taxed at less than half the regular rate. As a result, Wall Street CEOs sometimes pay a smaller percentage of their income as federal taxes than do many of the people working in their offices. During the heyday of the middle class economy, Federal income tax rates were many times higher for the rich. When President Reagan took office, the maximum federal tax rate was 70 percent. Even that was low compared to the 91 percent top rate during the 1950s. In fact, the last time our maximum Federal tax rate was as low as it is now was during the run-up to the Depression. During those years, the maximum rate was 25 percent. When Federal tax rates are cut, the middle class struggles to maintain the services they need. As a result, many of the shortfalls are passed along to states, then to local governments. Here, you find taxes that truly burden working people: sales taxes and property taxes. Compared to regular folks, wealthy people spend a much smaller part of their income buying clothes and groceries. A report released by the Institute on Taxation and Economic Policy in 2009 found that "every state and local tax system takes a much greater share of income from middle- and low-income families than from the wealthy."

When income flows naturally to most of the citizens, income redistribution through taxation is less necessary. The two principal areas most in need of attention are trade policy and labor laws. In decades past, American jobs and American markets were strongly protected by fair trade legislation. By the late 1980s, the movement toward "free trade" was gaining momentum and by now has completely overtaken our economic policy. The alphabet soup of WTO, NAFTA, CAFTA, leads to higher corporate profits and downward pressure on wages in the United States. This, in turn, causes further deterioration in our income distribution. We can't expect to maintain living wages for middle class workers in the face of studies like these:

- The Economic Policy Institute in 2011 found that a total of 682,900 U.S. jobs have been lost or displaced since 1994 as a result of the U.S. trade deficit with Mexico.

- Another Economic Policy Institute study, this one in 2010, found that our exploding trade deficit with China cost 2.4 million American jobs during 2001 to 2008.

A more enlightened approach to trade policy, one with the explicit goal of protecting our middle class society, would reduce the need for ensuing discussions of income redistribution. Instead, we have dozens of "think tanks" selling the story of how we will all be better off if our jobs go overseas, and a government that, judging by its actions, seems far too willing to go along with this economic pipedream.

The third over-riding factor affecting our income distribution is the weakening of labor unions. During the decades following World War II, the fraction of American workers represented by labor unions was several times larger than it is now. Furthermore, the laws protecting workers' rights to bargain for fair wages and decent working conditions were stronger and more effectively enforced than they are today. Labor unions, once strong enough to keep the gains from productivity in wages rather than corporate profits, are now too weak to do the job they once did. As a result, we see rising worker productivity without concurrent wage increases, a phenomenon relatively new in modern economic history. A study that appeared in the August 2011 issue of *The American Sociological Review* made clear the critical relationship between strong labor unions and a middle class economy. Declining labor union membership, according to the study, accounts for 20 percent of the increase in wage inequality among women and 33 percent of the wage inequality among men. The differences were beyond those that could be explained by education alone. As one of the study's authors noted, "For generations, unions were the core institution advocating for more equitable wage distribution."

In *Good Jobs America*, a book by Paul Osterman and Beth Shulman, a clear argument is made for not just any job, but jobs that will provide income that can support a family and allow them to prosper. As they so bluntly put it, "The gap between the low and middle class is collapsing." With the right policies, government can help make bad jobs into good ones. The work of Kris Jacobs and Kevin Ristau at the Minnesota Jobs Now Coalition makes it clear that raising the minimum wage would go a long way toward this end. The economy would improve as well when more money is put in the hands of those who will spend it.

Prof. William Darity of Duke University proposes "A Direct Route to Full Employment." His idea is that just as the Works Progress Administration and the Civilian Conservation Corps were used in the 1930s to put the unemployed back to work making things and providing services no one else would do, we should create a National Investment Employment Corps. This organization would encourage every local government, every school board, every county, and every state to submit proposals for all the jobs services they would like to provide but don't have the funds to make happen. They would apply to the agency for funds and hire the necessary employees. He points out that it would cost no more than the $1.3 trillion "too big to fail" handout to the investment banking community and would put to work the 15 million hands that were idle at the time he made his proposal. It would also be an investment that would pay back because workers pay taxes and contribute to the economy in far greater ways than they can subsisting on uncertain unemployment benefits.

This is similar to what Hyman Minsky proposed in the 1960s during President Johnson's war on poverty. The war on poverty proposed education, training, and welfare to bring the poor out of poverty. Minsky argued that without the commitment to provide jobs there was really little hope of moving people out of poverty. He proposed full employment by designating the government as the employer of last resort. He believed you needed to meet people where they were with a job (rather than trying to change them through education with the promise of a job) and give them a living wage. This would maintain and build their self respect and make them a productive part of society. His idea was to use some of the New Deal programs to put people to work. He emphasized jobs for those at the bottom rather than just high-skilled infra-structure work, which helped the high wage worker but didn't get those harder to place workers into the economy.

In the same vein, a Fellow of the World Policy Institute and the Century Foundation says, "If we do not begin to develop such policies, we will not have only the problem of runaway incomes for the few at the very top, but a large and growing part of the population—some of which is highly skilled and educated—that is cut off from the economy all together." Our government has moved in a direction where it no longer serves the interests of the vast majority. Something must be done that will change this, something that will address the environment of vulnerability our current system creates for the majority of working people and their families. A change in our basic contract and an institutional commitment to creating good jobs for working people will keep not only our economy moving, but will save our democracy.

The Minnesota State Legislature's signature accomplishment on moving toward living wage jobs was to raise the state's min-imum wage in 2014 for the first time in nearly ten years and approving automatic annual increases tied to the rate of infla-tion. Considering Minnesota was home to the third lowest min-imum wage ($6.15/hour) in the entire country, and one of only a handful below the federal minimum wage, this progress can-not be understated. When Minnesota's minimum wage increase is fully implemented to $9.50 per hour by 2016, over 350,000 Minnesotans will receive a raise and we will boast one of the highest minimum wages in the nation. Here is some demo-graphic information that gives us a better idea of who stands to benefit from the wage increase: 45 percent have some col-lege education; 57 percent are women; 62,850 are parents; and 14,200 are the sole wage earner in their household. While even this wage level does not provide the kind of economic security needed to build a middle class economy, it is an important step in the right direction. But $9.50 is meager compared to the $15 minimum wage that some cities are trying to put in place.

In addition to minimum wage workers, Minnesotans who care for seniors and people with disabilities, whether at home, in nursing homes or in other community-based settings, are some of the most grossly underpaid people in our workforce in spite of their physically and emotionally demanding jobs. This vital sector of our workforce is tasked with challenging jobs that will only become more and more demanding as the Baby Boomer generation retires and ages. Without a good wage, it's harder to retain these individuals and maintain consistent, high quality care for our seniors and people with disabilities. Our legislature provided nursing home employees and community-based health care providers with a five percent funding increase (and thereby a wage increase) after years of funding cuts and stagnant wages. Much like Minnesota's minimum wage workers, this modest increase does not provide the level of economic security individuals need to reach their full potential, but it represents a serious course correction. Let us all take hope that this is the first of many steps toward truly valuing the contributions of people who work.

I am especially proud of the Women's Economic Security Act that Minnesota passed in 2014. While the title of this legislation would leave one to believe it focuses exclusively on economic benefits for women, the goal is to improve economic security for working families overall. The law expands unpaid leave under the Minnesota Parental Leave Act from six to twelve weeks for both moms and dads and allows female employees to use unpaid leave for pregnancy-related needs. Employers are required to provide reasonable accommodations to an employee for health conditions related to pregnancy or childbirth; for example, a pregnant employee must be allowed more frequent restroom breaks, a water bottle at her work station, and the ability to sit while working. Female employees often discover pay inequities with their male counterparts in open discussions regarding pay; the law therefore prohibits employers from disciplining employees who openly discuss their pay and compensation. Businesses with state contracts must certify that they are in compliance with existing equal pay laws. And employees must not only be allowed to use existing earned sick leave to recover from sexual assault, domestic violence, or stalking, but those same circumstances must be considered when determining unemployment insurance eligibility. Efforts are now underway in the Minnesota Legislature to build upon the Women's Economic Security Act by moving to mandatory paid parental and sick leave, as well as predictable work schedules and additional workplace protections that help workers balance the responsibilities of work with those of family caregiving.

A commonly accepted definition of a Third World country is one that has virtually no middle class. The United States is on an economic path that slowly, but surely, will move us away from our middle class economy and toward one more closely resembling the extremes in an underdeveloped economy of rich and poor with few in the middle. It is time we woke up and realized that we cannot build a strong middle class on a foundation of cheap wages!

GETTING OUR PRIORITIES RIGHT

The Land of Opportunity

In my years in the Minnesota state legislature, I have noticed that everyone talks about saving our middle class economy, but many act in ways that do just the opposite. They cut education, defund health programs, let our roads fall apart, deny climate change, exempt polluters from regulations and support economic policies that have us working more for less. We are told we must go it alone, that our neighbor's problems have nothing to do with us. We are told to ignore Paul Wellstone's great advice: "We all do better when we all do better."

As we go down this road, more and more of us find that our neighbor's problems are now our problems. Our children don't have the schools we think they should, we worry more about health care, the roads we drive have more potholes, our climate is harsher, and our paycheck doesn't go as far as it used to. All of this adds up to shrinking opportunities, not just for us, but for our neighbors and our children. We find ourselves thinking that everyone deserves at least the opportunity for a good life, but wondering, "Where will those opportunities come from?"

Those opportunities come naturally for many who have the good fortune to live in a middle class economy. Others have been left behind because of the color of their skin, where they came from, or their gender. We must be clear that "all" means "all" and we can't bar some from opportunities to better themselves without ultimately harming everyone. Rebuilding and nurturing that concept must be front and center in our political action.

Tax breaks for the rich, small government, and ideological shouting matches simply cannot, and will not, get us where we need to be. What will get us there is restoring our priorities so that they are in line with the idea of opportunities for all. We must focus on the things we have to do together, not individual actions that may save some of us, but only at the expense of our neighbors and children. Those priorities are the five building blocks of a middle class society: education, health care, transportation, clean energy, and living wage jobs. Maintaining these foundations must be our number one legislative priority if we are to provide ourselves, our neighbors, and our children with the opportunities they deserve.

Notice that I have not been very specific about the exact actions we must take to advance our priorities. That is no accident. For one thing, actions that work in one part of the country may be different than those that work in another. For another, we shouldn't be deciding how we are going to get somewhere until we are sure we know where we are going. And, sadly, I don't think many of today's politicians know the right road is the one that leads to opportunity for all.

I can hear the objections already: "This is too expensive! Where will the money come from?" To those who raise such objections, we will have to remind them that our middle class economy was not lost overnight. That process began forty years ago and is still going on. We will have to remind them that so many years of not reinvesting in America will take time to correct. When people say "We can't afford this!" we'll also have to remind them that, even more so, we can't afford the alternative, that is, a Third World economy in which most of us lack for opportunity. That is not the American dream. This was not the intent of those who wrote our Constitution. And this is not a path that will lead us out of despair and into greatness. We are still the world's richest country. What we do with that great wealth and what policies can make better use of that wealth to continue to create opportunity and prosperity is everyone's business.

Changing the conversation about how we move forward and build and maintain a middle class economy is not an easy task. This is going to be a big job, far too big for any one of us, or even any one group of us, to get done on our own. All of us working together is a different story. We can renew our calling to build "a more perfect union" for all Americans. And we can live in a country where the words "The Land of Opportunity" truly mean something, not just for a privileged few, but also for each and every one of us.

Let's all do better! Together!

REFERENCES
AND
SUGGESTED
READINGS

Five Foundations

Beard, Charles A. *An Economic Interpretation of the Constitution of the United States* (1965). Free Press, New York.

Cassady, John. *How Markets Fail* (2009) Farrar Straus Giroux, New York.

Coggins, Jay, Thomas Legg and Dane Smith. "Widening Economic Inequality: Causes, Effects, and a Proposal for Estimating Its Impact in Policymaking." (2013) Growth and Justice. St. Paul.

Collins, Chuck, ed. *The Wealth Inequality Reader* (2004). Dollars & Sense Economic Affairs Bureau. Cambridge, MA.

Cummins, H. J. "Work & Life: Executives insulated from NWA pension fears" *StarTribune* August 10, 2005.

Eccles, Marriner S. *Beckoning Frontiers* (1951). Alfred A. Knopf. New York.

Frank, Robert H. *Falling Behind* (2007). University of California Press. Berkeley.

Frank, Robert H. and Philip J. Cook. *The Winner-Take-All Society* (1995). The Free Press. New York.

Friedman, Benjamin M. *The Moral Consequences of Economic Growth* (2005). Vintage Books. New York.

Galbraith, James K. *The Predator State* (2008.) Free Press. New York.

Galbraith, John Kenneth. *The Crash of 1929* (2009). Mariner Books. Boston, MA.

Garfinkle, Norton. *The American Dream vs. The Gospel of Wealth: The Fight for a Productive Middle-Class Economy* (2006). Yale University Press. New Haven.

Garson, Barbara. *Down the Up Escalator* (2013). Random House. New York.

Hacker, Jacob S. and Paul Pierson. *Winner Take All Politics* (2010). Simon and Schuster. New York.

Hartmann, Thom. *Screwed: The Undeclared War Against the Middle Class* (2006). Barret-Koehler Publishing. San Francisco.

Morgenstern, Gretchen and Joshua Rosner. *Reckless Endangerment* (2011). Times Books, Henry Holt and Co. New York.

Moyers, Bill. *Moyers on Democracy* (2008). Doubleday. New York.

Phillips, Kevin. *Bad Money* (2008). Viking. New York.

Phillips-Fein, Kim. *Invisible Hands: The Businessmen's Crusade Against the New Deal* (2009). W.W. Norton. New York.

Putnam, Robert D. *Bowling Alone* (2000). Simon and Schuster. New York.

Reich, Robert. *Aftershock: The Next Economy and America's Future* (2010). Alfred A. Knopf. New York.

Saul, John Ralston. *The Unconscious Civilization* (1995). Free Press. New York.

Schultz, Ellen E. *Retirement Heist* (2011). Portfolio/Penguin. New York.

Stiglitz, Joseph E. *Freefall* (2010). W.W. Norton Company. New York.

Sunstein, Cass R. *The Second Bill of Rights: FDR's Unfinished Revolution and Why We Need It More Than Ever* (2004). Basic Books. New York.

Veblen, Thorstein B. *The Theory of the Business Enterprise* (1904). Charles Scribner's and Sons. New York.

Wilkinson, Richard and Kate Picket. *The Spirit Level* (2009). Bloomsbury Press. New York.

EDUCATION

Barr, Robert D. and William H. Parrett. *Saving Our Schools, Saving Our Students* (2003). Skylight Professional Development. Glenview, Illinios.

Brown, Phillip, Hugh Lauder, and David Ashton. *The Global Auction* (2011). Oxford Univ. Press. Oxford, UK.

Christensen, Clayton M. *Disrupting Class* (2008). McGraw Hill. New York.

Deming, W. Edwards. *The New Economics for Industry, Government, Education* (1993). MIT Press. Cambridge, MA.

Erikson, Erik H. *Childhood and Society* (1950). W.W. Norton & Co. New York.

Folbre, Nancy. "What Makes Teachers Productive?" *New York Times*, September 19, 2011.

Gatto, John Taylor. *The Underground History of American History* (2001). The Oxford Village Press. New York.

Giroux, Henry A. "Beyond the Swindle of the Corporate University: Higher Education in the Service of Democracy." *Truthout*, January 18, 2011.

Glines, Don. *Declaring War Against Schooling* (2012). Rowman & Littlefield Education. Plymouth, UK.

Holt, John. *How Children Fail* (1964). Dell Publishing. New York.

Kohn, Alfie. *Feel-Bad Education* (2011). Beacon Press. Boston, MA.

Kohn, Alfie. *What Does It Mean to Be Well Educated?* (2004). Beacon Press. Boston, MA.

Meier, Deborah. *Will Standards Save Public Education?* Beacon Press. Boston, MA

Meier, Deborah. *In Schools We Trust* (2002). Beacon Press. Boston, MA.

Meier, Deborah and George Wood, eds. *Many Children Left Behind* (2004). Beacon Press. Boston, MA.

Mintz, Jerry and Carlo Ricci, eds. *Turning Points: 35 Visionaries in Education Tell Their Stories* (2010). Alternative Education Resource Organization, Inc. Roslyn Heights, NY.

Mosley, Walter. *Twelve Steps Toward a Political Revelation* (2011). Nation Books. New York.

Mosley, Walter. *Life out of Context* (2006). Nation Books. New York.

Pink, Daniel. *Drive: The Surprising Truth About What Motivates Us* (2009). Riverhead Books. New York.

Putnam, Robert D. *Our Kids: The American Dream in Crisis* (2015). Simon and Schuster. New York.

Ravitch, Diane. *Left Back: A Century of Battles Over School Reform* (2000). Touchstone Books. New York.

Ravitch, Diane. *The Death and Life of the Great American School System: How Testing and Choice Are Undermining Education* (2010). Basic Books. New York.

Rose, Mike. *Lives on The Boundary* (1989). Penguin Books. New York.

Schmickle, Sharon. "What's Happening to Minnesota's Higher-Ed Commitment?" MINNPOST, May 12, 2009.

Smith, Dane, et al. *Smart Investments in Minnesota's Students: A Research-Based Investment Proposal* (2008). Growth and Justice. St. Paul.

Stoddard, Lynn. *Educating for Human Greatness* (2010). Holistic Education Press. Brandon, VT.

Tucker, Marc S. "Standing on the Shoulders of Giants: An American Agenda for Education Reform." National Center on Education and the Economy. May 24, 2011.

Health care

Johnston, David Cay. *Free Lunch* (2007). Portfolio, Penguin Group. New York.

Lang, Amy. *Beyond the Affordable Act: An Economic Analysis of a Unified System of Health Care for Minnesota* (2012). Growth and Justice. St. Paul.

Lieberman, Trudy. "Wrong Prescription? The failed promise of the ACA" *Harper's Magazine*, July 2015.

Potter, Wendell. *Deadly Spin* (2010). Bloomsbury Press. New York.

Reid, T.R. *The Healing of America* (2009). The Penguin Press. New York.

Sullivan, Kip. *The Health Care Mess: How We Got into It and How We'll Get Out of It* (2006). Author House. Bloomington, IN.

Transportation

Ambrose, Stephen. *Nothing Like It in the World* (2001). Simon and Schuster. New York.

Condon, Patrick M. *Seven Rules for Sustainable Communities* (2010). Island Press. Washington.

Gordon, J.E. *Structures: Or Why Things Don't Fall Down* (1986). Da Capo Press. New York.

Heilbroner, Robert and Aaron Singer. *The Economic Transformation of America* (1994). Harcourt Brace College Publishers. Fort Worth.

Kane, Matt. *Smart Investments in Transportation for Minnesota: Goals and Targets to Spur Growth and Expand Prosperity* (2011). Growth and Justice. St. Paul.

Madrick, Jeff. *The Case for Big Government* (2011). Princeton University Press. Princeton, NJ.

Pursell, Carroll W. *Technology in America: A History of Individuals and Ideas* (1981). The MIT Press. Cambridge, MA.

Simmons, Matthew R. *Twilight in the Desert* (2005). John Wiley & Sons. Hoboken, NJ.

Sinclair, Upton. *The Flivver King: A Story of Ford-America* (1937). Charles Kerr Publishing Co. Chicago.

ENERGY SYSTEMS

Casper, Barry M. and Paul David Wellstone. *Powerline: The First Battle of America's Energy War* (1981). University of Massachusetts Press. Amherst.

Ditmore, Jack and Dane Smith. *Action Without Regrets in a Climate of Uncertainty: Smart Investments with Immediate Benefits.* Growth and Justice. St. Paul.

Friedman, Julio. "Why it is hard to talk about energy." *Atlantic Monthly*, March 29, 2011.

Friedman, Thomas L. *Hot, Flat, and Crowded* (2008). Farrar Straus and Giroux; New York.

Gardner, Gary. *Creating Sustainable Prosperity in the United States: The Need for Innovation and Leadership* (2011). Worldwatch Institute. Washington DC.

Hawken, Paul. *The Ecology of Commerce* (1993). Harper Collins. New York.

Hawken, Paul. *Blessed Unrest* (2007). Viking. New York.

Hawken, Paul, Amory Lovins, and L. Hunter Lovins. *Natural Capitalism* (1999). Little, Brown and Co. Boston.

Inslee, Jay and Bracken Hendricks. *Apollo's Fire* (2008). Island Press. Washington.

Johnston, David Cay. "Fiscal Therapy." *Mother Jones*, Jan./Feb. 2009.

Kennedy, Robert F., Jr. *Crimes Against Nature* (2004). Harper Collins. New York.

Larson, Jonathan. *Elegant Technology: Economic Prosperity from an Economic Blueprint* (1992). The Riverdale Co. Westwood, MA.

Makhijani, Arjun. *Carbon-Free and Nuclear-Free: A Roadmap for U.S. Energy Policy* (2007). RDR Books and IEER Press. Takoma Park, MD and Muskegon, MI.

Mark, Michael van, ed. *Electricity from Renewable Energy Sources* (2008). Federal Ministry for the Environoment, Nature Conservation and Nuclear Safety. Berlin.

Mendonca, Miguel. *Feed-in Tariffs* (2007). Earthscan. London.

Morris, David; "The Real American Exceptionalism" Huffington Post. April 20, 2011.

Morris, David.; *Self-Reliant Cities* (1982). Sierra Club Books. San Francisco.

Morris, David. *Seeing the Light* (2001). Institute for Local Self-Reliance. Minneapolis.

Palast, Greg. *Vulture's Picnic* (2011). Dutton. New York.

Palast, Greg, Jerrold Oppenheim, and Theo MacGregor. *Democracy and Regulation* (2003). Pluto Press. London.

Rickerson, Wilson and Robert C. Grace. *The Debate Over Fixed Price Incentives for Renewable Electricity in Europe and the United States* (2007). Heinrich Boll Foundation. Washington DC.

Roberts, Paul Craig. *How the Economy Was Lost* (2010). Counterpunch and AK Press. Oakland, CA.

Senge, Peter. *The Necessary Revolution* (2008). Doubleday. New York.

Acuff, Stewart and Richard A. Levins. *Getting America Back to Work* (2010). Tasora Books. Minneapolis.

Bageant, Joe. *Deer Hunting with Jesus* (2008). Crown Publishing Group. New York.

Belz, Adam. "Workers' Aspirations Stagnate with Pay." *StarTribune*, February 15, 2015.

Brouwer, Steve. *Robbing Us Blind* (2004). Common Courage Press. Monroe, ME.

Coles, Robert. *Lives of Moral Leadership* (2000). Random House. New York.

Dorgan, Byron. *Take this Job and Ship It* (2006). St. Martin's Press. New York.

Dulles, Foster Rhea and Melvyn Dubofsky. *Labor in America* (1996). Harlan Davidson, Inc. Wheeling, Illinois.

Glickman, Lawrence B. *A Living Wage* (1997). Cornell University Press. Ithaca, NY.

Granholm, Jennifer. *A Governor's Story* (2011). Public Affairs. New York.

Galbraith, John Kenneth. *American Capitalism* (1956). Riverside Press. Cambridge, MA.

Heilbronner, Robert L. *Beyond Boom and Crash* (1978). W. W. Norton and Co. New York.

Herbert, Bob. *Losing Our Way: An Intimate Portrait of a Troubled America* (2014). Doubleday. New York.

Jobs Now Coalition. "2010 Cost of Living Report" St. Paul, MN.

Jobs Now Coalition. "Wage Calculator" St. Paul, MN.

Johnston, Robert D. *The Radical Middle Class* (2003). Princeton University Press. Princeton, NJ.

Miller, Matthew. *The 2% Solution* (2003). Public Affairs. New York.

Minsky, Hyman P. *Ending Poverty: Jobs, Not Welfare* (2013). Levy Economics Institute. Annandale on Hudson, NY.

Mondale, Walter. *The Good Fight* (2010). Scribner. New York.

Packer, George. "The Broken Contract." *Foreign Affairs*, Nov./Dec. 2011.

Perkins, Frances. *The Roosevelt I Knew* (2011). Penguin Books. New York.

Reich, Robert. "The Roughed Up American." Washington Post, September 14, 2014.

Sanders, Bernie. *The Speech* (2011). Nation Books. New York.

A TIME FOR ACTION

"Inequality for All." (2013) A film with Robert Reich and directed by Jacob Kornbluth. 72 Productions.

In a time when most churches are embracing short-term strategies for short-term results, Dean Niforatos and Ron Auch have put forth a thought provoking and spiritually challenging work. They dare to ask not what do the people want, but what does God want in our church's worship, preaching, and doctrine? How does He judge our success? Both Dean and Ron write in a bold style that reflects their passionate pursuit of God's Spirit and souls for over 20 years. Whether pastor or parishioner you will find this book both interesting and spiritually enriching.

Reece Bowling, Senior Pastor,
Orchard Road Christian Center, Denver, CO
Executive Vice President,
Marilyn Hickey Ministries

As an evangelist I have seen the message of The Jesus-Sensitive Church *fleshed out both nationally and internationally. I began reading on a flight over the Pacific . . . and could not put the manuscript down. Pentecostal churches need to read and carefully consider the message and the implications of this book. I endorse it as one who is watching it happen!*

Mike Livengood
Mike Livengood Ministries, Danville, Illinois

The Jesus-Sensitive Church *is a clear, clarion call back to Christ, the power of the baptism in the Holy Spirit, and ministry according to the operations manual — the Word of God. A message the church desperately needs to hear today.*

Bill Juoni, Evangelist, Whitewater, WI

This book will give you more passion for Jesus. In a day when there are so many things "pulling" on us — including religion — we need a fresh focus on Jesus. I like this book; as I read the manuscript, I asked the Lord to help me not to get caught up in methodology, but caught up in Jesus. Jesus is the only one who loved us all enough to die for us. If you want a book to challenge you, to push you out of your rut, I am certain you, too, will appreciate and enjoy this book.

Marilyn Hickey
Author and conference speaker, Denver, CO

THE JESUS SENSITIVE CHURCH

WHERE WOULD JESUS WORSHIP?

RON AUCH
DEAN NIFORATOS

First printing: July 2006

ISBN-13: 978-0-89221-657-4
ISBN-10: 0-89221-657-3
Library of Congress Catalog Number: 2006928474

Cover by Left Coast Design, Portland, Oregon

All Scripture is from the New International Version of the Bible, unless otherwise noted.

Printed in the United States of America

For information regarding author interviews, please contact the publicity department at (870) 438-5288.

Please visit our website for other great titles:
www.newleafpress.net

New Leaf Press
A Division of New Leaf Publishing Group

Contents

CHAPTER 1

THE JESUS-SENSITIVE CHURCH

WHERE WOULD JESUS WORSHIP? If Jesus still lived on this earth, would He worship at your church? I imagine every pastor believes that Jesus would attend his church, if He were here. Would He really? It seems that Jesus and His standards have become an offense to many Christians today.

Ron writes: Lets face it; the church in America is in trouble. We may have more mega-churches than we've ever had, but we also have fewer people going to church than ever before. In Tom Clegg's book *Lost in America*, he cites "Seven Deadly Statistics."[1] I will paraphrase them here.

1. The percentage of adults in the United States who attend church is decreasing.

WHERE
WOULD
JESUS
WORSHIP?

2. Roughly half of all churches in America did not add one new person through conversion growth last year.

3. No matter how you do the math, current conversion rates still point to one horrible conclusion: lost people lose.

4. Some researchers claim that more churches are closing than are opening every year.

5. Conversions to other religions and dropouts from Christianity are escalating.

6. The decline in Christianity has been going on for nearly 50 years.

7. Too many churched people believe and behave identically to their unchurched counterparts.

This is just the beginning. There are many more staggering facts that we need to deal with, such as: Atheists are less likely to become divorced than are Christians. On American soil, every other religion is gaining converts while Christianity is losing them. The unchurched population of the United States is the largest mission field in the English-speaking world and the fifth largest globally. I highly recommend the book *Lost in America* by Tom Clegg and Warren Bird, if you are at all interested in what is happening with the church in America.

The Jesus-Sensitive Church is not a book about church growth. It's about church philosophy and, more specifically,

Pentecostal church philosophy. Enough books have been written about church growth already. If even one of them actually worked, there would be no need for another one. It's this author's belief that the Pentecostal church in America needs to seriously look at where it's headed in our society. We are a movement that seems to be desperately grasping at anything to breathe life back into it.

Consider this; the largest churches in the world are all Spirit-filled, and yet the Pentecostal pastors of America are clamoring for the advice and expertise of men who know very little about the moving of the spirit, men who even belittle the third person of the Trinity. We seem to be desperate to have these men teach us how to grow our churches.

Pastor David Cho from Seoul, Korea, the pastor of the largest church in the world (800,000-plus members), could break off ten percent of his current congregation to start a new church and he would still have a church four times the size of the biggest churches in America. Nigeria, Africa, is home to the second largest church in the world. It has 650,000 Spirit-filled congregants. India has an Assemblies of God church that numbers well over 100,000 members. Brazil has many Spirit-filled churches that far outnumber the largest evangelical churches in America. In light of all of these facts, the "Spirit-filled" pastors in America have somehow come to believe that their greatest opportunity for church growth will be found within the evangelical, seeker-sensitive, non-Pentecostal, approach.

We are allowing those who know very little about the Holy Spirit to dictate our approach to doing church. The seeker-sensitive philosophy is diametrically opposed to what used to be the Spirit-controlled, Spirit-led way of doing church.

Just think of it — we are the people that believe in the gifts of the Spirit. We believe in the value of the flow of the Spirit. We are tongue talkers and yet, in America, when it comes to doing church, we turn to those who do not hold to our theological perspectives at all. We stand in the shadow of our Pentecostal brothers and sisters around the world, who have the biggest and fastest growing churches, who all attribute their success to prayer and the moving of God's Spirit, and yet somehow we believe we will be able to come up with another key to success.

Years ago, Pastor Cho made a statement to a group of ministers about prayer. He said that when he teaches a pastors' conference in the United States and talks about cell groups, the notebooks fly open and they write down everything he says. However, when he would come to the subject of prayer, the very subject that he credits the growth of his church to, he said the pastors would quietly close their notebooks, fold their hands, and politely wait for him to get off the subject. Cho believes that American pastors are spiritually blind to their need to pray. They simply can't see it. Is it possible that Cho's comments about the American pastor and his inability to see that prayer is the answer is true? Are we truly blind to this?

LOOKING FOR TRUTH

We have a wonderful opportunity to present to the youth of today exactly what they are looking for. There is a spirit in the world today, amongst our young people, that is very similar to the spirit which was in our world back in the 1960s when the hippie movement came into being and ushered in the current drug culture. Our young people today are becoming more and more discontent with society. They don't believe they can trust anybody. Every aspect of "the establishment" seems corrupt. Unfortunately, the organized church, in their eyes, is a part of "the establishment." But is that really true? Do they simply reject the organized church, or do they reject what they see in the organized church in America? Around the world, the organized church is doing great.

"BreakPoint" with Chuck Colson ran a very interesting story about this very thing. Consider the following quote.

> When it comes to Islamic conversions, you can't help but count the ironies. Throughout history, Islam has spread through violent conquest. Today — after Islamic radicals killed thousands of our fellow Americans — Americans are voluntarily converting. Another irony: Around the country, so-called "seeker friendly" churches try to attract people through pop music and sanctuaries that resemble shopping malls. Meanwhile, Islam — which just

suffered a huge public relations debacle — attracts converts through what can only be described as seeker unfriendly elements: rigid rules of conduct, dress, and life.

Islam is now the fastest growing religion in the United States. More than 30 percent of mosque attendees are converts. What is going on? Well, first of all, the terrorists' attacks have sparked an interest in learning more about Islam, a religion that appears exotic to Western eyes. Secondly, during times of crisis, religions with clear definitions of right and wrong look increasingly attractive. Karen Courtenay, one of the new converts who gathered at the Old Country Buffet, told *National Post* that many converts are attracted to "Islam's rich mysticism and clear theology and rules," its family values, sense of community, and moral certainty. Some — especially Hispanic and African Americans — view the embrace of Islam as a return to their roots.[2]

That is an amazing story — especially in light of the prevailing philosophy of how we should go about growing our churches. If we are wise, we will see this as our opportunity to go back to preaching it straight. The very fact that young people are converting to Islam should speak volumes to us. They are looking for structure and a rigidity that they cannot find in the church today, everything about many churches today is slick and polished — and then when they do go to church they can easily spot the "bait-and-switch" tactics of the seeker-sensitive church. They are not impressed with our ability to be slick.

The only people we are impressing with our easy gospel is ourselves. Transfer growth is almost our only hope of growing our own churches. Christians are running to the biggest show in town, but not the non-Christians. They want the simple truth, and we seem to be running from it as fast as we can. I'm not talking about our theology — I'm talking about our philosophy of ministry.

When I planted Prayer House, the Lord laid it on my heart to call our church a "Jesus-sensitive church." In a "Jesus-sensitive church" we want Jesus to be very comfortable, we do not want Him to be offended by anything we say, and we make His desires the primary thrust of the church. I don't believe there is anyone more sensitive to the needs of those who are seeking than Jesus. When did we ever get it in our heads that we had to protect the seeker from Jesus? When did the presence of God become inadequate to do the work of God? What the seeker needs is a real, living sense of the presence of God. People simply need to feel Jesus. They need an encounter with Him, and that is not going to happen without a strong sense of His presence in our services.

We are quickly falling into a "the end justifies the means" mindset. The growing trend in our churches is to have coffee shops to draw people in. Many churches are singing the praises of "Starbucks," while at the same time breathing a sigh of relief that finally we have found something to help us get people into churches.

Many people want the freedom to sip a hot cup of coffee and simultaneously be casual and comfortable during the Sunday morning worship service. Church cafes are growing and drawing people to church. Is there anything wrong with a coffee shop in a church? No! There is nothing wrong with it at all. But why stop there? If it's merely a matter of getting people in the front door of the church, why not have each of the female greeters wear a Hooters outfit? That should draw people in also. As long as we are no longer depending upon the Holy Spirit to draw people, we could do anything that works since we think the end justifies the means.

I don't want us to throw away our heritage of dependency upon the Holy Spirit. Pentecostal churches used to be known for their vibrant worship, their Spirit-filled preachers, their openness to the gifts of the Spirit, their fire, and their audience participation. Today we sit in cushioned chairs sipping coffee while we watch a video of the pastor. That may be good for other churches but it is diametrically opposed to the traditional Pentecostal method of doing church.

THE PREACHER'S PRAYER LIFE

"There is today no lack of Bible teachers to set forth correctly the principles of the doctrines of Christ, but too many of these seem satisfied to teach the fundamentals of the faith year after year, strangely unaware that there is in their ministry no manifest presence, nor anything unusual in their personal lives. They minister constantly to believers who feel within their breasts a longing, which their teaching simply does not satisfy."[3]

It's my contention that the reason we don't see much of the manifest presence of God in our services is because of the lack of time preachers spend in His presence. Many preachers do not have a prayer life. Don't make the mistake of thinking that having prayer in your life is the same as having a prayer life. I think all preachers have some element of prayer in their lives. All of us, if nothing else, are forced to pray from time to time, but there is a major difference between having an element of prayer in your life and having a life and ministry centered around prayer.

The former revivalist Leonard Ravenhill used to have the habit of spending the first four hours of his day in prayer. He told his secretary to not interrupt him from 8:00 a.m. until 12:00 p.m. Rev. David Cho spends at least two to three hours in private prayer daily. You can hardly name a great man of God without associating his ministry with prayer.

Not too many years ago, the evangelical church was looking at us and asking why our churches were growing so fast. We had many wonderful opportunities to tell them about the empowering ability of the Holy Spirit. This is still the case in most mission fields — not so in America today. Today we have become sophisticated. We have moved beyond the "old" days and ways into what simply seems to be a "daze." We don't know where we are going. We don't know what model to follow. Subsequently, we have a mixture of evangelical, high-church, Pentecostal, and legalistic philosophies, all trying to guide us at the same time. There is some good in all of them but when you try to mix them all into the same church you will end up with a confused congregation at best.

If we are Pentecostal, then let's be Pentecostal. If you are evangelical, then be evangelical. Don't try to be whatever seems to be the "latest thing" unless it fits within your philosophy of ministry. Churches are different because they share different philosophies. I don't believe God wants all churches to look alike. Churches are different for a reason. Before I create too much of a negative image of the seeker-sensitive church let me clarify something. It is very possible that they are meeting a need in our society today; however, the Pentecostal church was never meant to be the kind of church that needs to look to all sorts of different gadgets and means to grow its churches. We honor the ministry of the Holy Spirit because He makes Jesus so real to us, and Jesus is all anybody really needs to experience.

One of the cornerstone verses in the Pentecostal church is Acts 1:8:

> But you will receive power when the Holy
> Spirit comes on you; and you will be my witnesses

in Jerusalem, and in all Judea and Samaria, and to the ends of the earth.

Unfortunately, today the biggest boost many people get from church comes from a coffee cup. Maybe that's why Jesus said, "My Father, if it is possible, may this *cup* be taken from me" (Matt. 26:39). Jesus saw the trend and was "stirring" clear of it (bad joke).

IT'S MY FAMILY'S FAULT!

Dean writes: As an evangelist who has traveled nationally and internationally for over 20 years, I have seen the drastic difference between what I like to call "Churchianity" (church done with the sincerest efforts of well-meaning men) and true, first-century Christianity (or as Ron and I like to call it, "Jesus-sensitive" Christianity).

As I prayed and fasted much regarding this book, I realized it is all my family's fault for the relatively power-less state of the Church in America! I take the blame! Let me explain.

IT STARTED WITH GREAT, GREAT, GREAT GRANDDAD

Being of Greek descent, I am related to many of America's restaurant owners, and also to the man whose thought is in many ways the foundation of our Western Civilization. His name was Aristotle, a great philosopher, and unlike many Greeks, not a particularly good cook.

Aristotle's basic philosophy stated that the only things in this world that are real are those things which we perceive through our senses. If we cannot see, hear, touch, taste, or smell something, it is not "real." This philosophy is the foundation of rationalistic, scientific Western thought. The creed of this is: "If I see it, I will believe it!"

This philosophy found its way into the Church over the centuries. The result is a religion whose central pillar is the death and resurrection of the "God-man," but a constituency that doesn't believe in anything that goes beyond their reason or senses.

Hence, we have too many Christians in America who profess much, but possess little. They lay claim to the Bible as the Word of God, but don't really believe its testimonies of miracles, healings, and deliverances from demons. The result is a faith that is merely a philosophy of life and not an expected powerful encounter with a supernatural God as Jesus told His disciples to expect in Luke 24:49 and Acts 1:8.

The byproduct of all this in America is two-fold:

1. We preach a gospel that does not offend our "intelligence." In other words, we try not to imply that we believe in things science cannot explain. (Note all the TV programs today that try to give scientific credence to things we used to proudly declare we believed simply because God said it.)

2. If we admit to the gifts and power of the Holy Spirit and the supernatural, we allocate those who desire to pursue them into a backroom somewhere with the instruction that

God never meant these things to happen in front of the lost because it would turn them off.

How can we have come to this when the Bible gives us a history of an early church that openly prayed in tongues in front of crowds of lost people (Acts 2), healed the sick in public places (Acts 3), cast out devils in a business atmosphere (Acts 16), and even saw *church membership roles purged by the killing off of those who lied to the Holy Spirit* (Acts 5), and all this while seeing nothing but the church grow, grow, grow?

We have come to this because we have accepted Aristotle's philosophy, which is the foundation of all the church growth methods in America. We have been reduced to an intellectual, philosophical, practical, needs-based faith, and we Pentecostals have bought this lie of the devil hook, line, and sinker!

Endnotes

1. Tom Clegg and Warren Bird, *Lost in America: How You and Your Church Can Impact the World Next Door* (Loveland, CO: Group, 2001).

2. "BreakPoint" with Chuck Colson, Commentary #020130 (January 30, 2002).

3. A.W. Tozer, *The Pursuit of God* (Camp Hill, PA: Christian Publications, 1982), p. 9.

CHAPTER 2

GIVE THEM
WHAT THEY WANT!

WHERE WOULD JESUS WORSHIP? Would He worship at your church if, in fact, your church is primarily concerned about meeting the carnal needs of the parishioner more so than their spiritual needs?

Ron writes: One of our not-too-distant presidents popularized a style of leadership which, through polls, basically gave the American people whatever they wanted. Many of the president's defenders, when confronted with this style of leadership, would say, "But the American people want _____ (you can fill in the blank)." I started giving this some serious thought after reading a book about church growth. It seems many pastors have adapted a similar style of leadership. The author of the book I read has one of the most progressive churches in the country. It is growing by leaps and bounds.

WHERE
WOULD
JESUS
WORSHIP?

In an effort to get his church to grow, this pastor would take polls amongst his people and then, in essence, give them what they wanted. One example of this was the way they chose their worship music. They had been very traditional in their choice of music, but felt their people were not really getting into it. They decided to ask everybody in the church to give them the call letters of their favorite local radio stations. They found out that the overwhelming majority of his congregation listened to soft rock or adult contemporary music. They made the adjustment and began to play that style of music in their worship services. They found that to be a key in church growth for them. They began to grow at an unprecedented rate.

I struggle with this. First of all, doesn't it seem that something is out of order to find that most of the people in the church are listening to secular music as their favorite type of music? As a shepherd and spiritual guide, shouldn't that be a red flag? Shouldn't that pastor have said, "We have a problem here! We have people that have very little spiritual depth. They spend more time listening to music that does not glorify God than music that does."

Whatever happened to the idea of Christians filling their minds with things above, not things upon the earth? Was the apostle Paul really serious when he said, "Set your minds on things above, not on earthly things" (Col. 3:2)?

Instead of this pastor seeing this as a problem, he saw it as an opportunity. In essence, he said: If that is what they want, that is what we will provide them. Give the sheep what they want.

TWO TYPES OF MINISTERS

The prophet Ezekiel ran into a similar problem in his day. There were two types of ministers (priests) leading God's people during his day. One type was willing to accommodate Israel in her worldliness, the other was not.

Ezekiel 44:6–7 says:

> Say to the rebellious house of Israel, "This is what the Sovereign LORD says: Enough of your detestable practices, O house of Israel! In addition to all your other detestable practices, you brought foreigners uncircumcised in heart and flesh into my sanctuary, desecrating my temple while you offered me food, fat and blood, and you broke my covenant."

The first group of Levites allowed individuals with uncircumcised hearts into the sanctuary. An uncircumcised heart is a heart full of fleshly/worldly desires. The Levites were the priestly family. They were appointed to serve God as ministers in His sanctuary. However, a group of them had become worldly and subsequently allowed an idolatrous Israel to bring her idols (fleshliness) into the sanctuary. We must note here that there is a great difference between bringing people into the church who need Christ and accommodating people in their sin. The problem was not that the priests allowed foreigners into the sanctuary as much as it was that they had no intention of changing them. They were compliant with them.

Ezekiel 44:10–13 states:

> The Levites who went far from me when Israel went astray and who wandered from me after their idols must bear the consequences of their sin. . . . They are not to come near to serve me as priests or come near any of my holy things or my most holy offerings; they must bear the shame of their detestable practices.

God punished them for accommodating Israel in her idolatry. What's interesting about this is that these priests were allowed to continue in the ministry. They were allowed to serve God in the sanctuary. However, they were no longer allowed to come near to God himself. They were not allowed to come near the "holy things."

The second group of Levites was of a different mindset. Ezekiel 44:15-16:

> But the priests, who are Levites and descendants of Zadok and who faithfully carried out the duties of my sanctuary when the Israelites went astray from me, are to come near to minister before me; they are to stand before me to offer sacrifices of fat and blood, declares the Sovereign LORD. They alone are to enter

my sanctuary; they alone are to come near my table
to minister before me and perform my service.

The second group of priests did not accommodate Israel
in her worldliness. They maintained God's holy standard,
and subsequently they were able to minister to God himself. They alone could enter into the Holy of Holies. Their
attitude would have been the opposite of the first group
of priests. Instead of saying, "Give the people what they
want," they would have said, "What does God want us to
give these people?"

One of my concerns is that it seems the Church today
has become content with a vibrant church service whether
or not the presence of God is there. Large crowds do not
automatically guarantee the presence of God. That is determined by holiness. The level of holiness is determined
by the amount of separation in a person's life. If a pastor
has accommodated the worldliness of the church today, he
may have a big crowd but he will be hard pressed to find
the presence of God there.

But the People Want . . . !

I once heard a man say, "There is a reason why the people
of God are called sheep. Sheep must be led." Sheep need a
shepherd. They cannot lead themselves because they lack
common sense. If sheep are in a pasture they will eat all the
grass available to them. Once the grass is gone, instead of
knowing that they should move on to the next pasture, they

will begin to eat their own waste. Eventually, all types of disease sets in. Without a shepherd, they will destroy themselves. The nuts are not to run the nut house. They don't know what is best for them. Yet that is exactly what is happening in our churches where they have the attitude that what the people want is what we should give them. No wonder there is so much disease and filth in the church today.

What is going to happen to a church that gives the people what they want rather than actually shepherding them into spirituality? The problem is, when we rule by popular vote, we no longer have a standard. The Constitution is the standard rule of law in our country. We are to base our legal decisions upon its rules and regulations. When a president rules according to what the people want rather than the Constitution, initially he will be very popular. However, the day will come when we look back and say, "How did we get to where we are today? There is no rule of law. The people are doing exactly what they want to do." That's anarchy.

J. Konrad Hölè, pastor of Life Changers Church North America, in the Twin Cities of Minneapolis/St. Paul in Minnesota, is saying some very interesting and important things to the Church today. In his publication *The World-view Leader*, he is suggesting that we take a serious look at where we are headed as a Church. We must ask ourselves what the Church will look like 100 years from now if it remains dependant upon gimmicks. What will happen if no wonderful new authors come along with a plan for the perfect church? What kind of disciples will we have if they are not being led from one pasture to another?

Hölè writes:

> When the American church is bigger, but American culture is worse, then something is tragically wrong. . . . The American church has got to do something far more profound to prepare for upcoming decades than simply comprising the God-fearing "red states."
>
> It is our complete void of a biblical world view that prevents us from creating a line upon line strategy that could serve as the backdrop for the type of reformation that would dwarf issues of moral lawlessness — a world view that would give us a more functional and dominant place in history. It is a voice that current end-time Bible prophecy decoders, zuit-suit televangelists, and Jesus in a happy meal mega-church CEOs, seem too enamored with their own place in ministry to give us.

Hölè goes on to talk about where the church is headed. He says the church today has become a "hooker church."

> The church was the place where we preached that God could clean up a harlot. Now, we have become one. Due to the result of a weak world view we have

created a form of church that is reminiscent of a street corner hooker. Not the inexperienced hooker who gets used one time and then gets rescued by someone with compassion for her pain and perversion. Rather, the Hooker Church, like a veteran prostitute, turns one trick, takes her profit, and waits for another John to come along and exploit her potential and co-dependence all over again.

We keep waiting on the corner for one move after the other. Another wave, another Toronto blessing, or Pensacola revival. The restoration wave, then the spiritual warfare wave, then the prophetic wave. Now, it is the return of the Apostles. Some of the churches I have spoken in were so consumed with "everything prophetic," I almost wondered if they wore apostolic or prophetic undergarments, too. After all, the Mormons do! And they also believe in Apostles and Prophets![1]

By the Book

For many years, Sears was the biggest store of its type in America. It started out similarly to Wal-Mart in that it was a very popular discount store. Sears was a major player for many years in the world market. After some time, another store in the Chicago area started up as a competitor to Sears. It was called Nordstrom's. As Nordstrom's grew, Sears began to lose a large part of the market to Nordstrom's. Eventually

Nordstrom's began to gross more in sales, in the Chicago area, than Sears.

A news reporter was dispatched to do a story about the two stores and try to figure out why Sears was losing out to Nordstrom's. A meeting was set up for the two CEOs to meet and talk about what was happening with their corporations. The meeting room had a lot of tension as all the parties took their seats in the headquarters building of Nordstrom's with the two CEOs sitting across from each other.

The moderator began by asking the CEO of Nordstrom's what he attributed his success to. The CEO immediately got up and left the room. The moderator was quite embarrassed. He wondered if he had asked the wrong question. Suddenly the door of the room re-opened and Nordstrom's CEO returned. He sat down and placed a book on the table. Then he said, "Our success has come from following this book to the letter." When asked what book he was referring to, he held up a very tattered copy of the original operations manual from the Sears Corporation. Looking the CEO from Sears square in the eyes, he continued, "We did it exactly the way you said it should be done. We did it according to the book."

It seems we are having a problem simply doing it like the Book says. We have come to believe that today's societal needs transcend the Bible's answers. In the church, the Bible is our standard. Pastors are not to lead according to what the people want. They are to lead according to what God wants. We are seeing the same thing happening in our churches today that we are seeing in the world. It's called "leadership by consensus," which amounts to no leadership at all.

STILL MINISTER

Let's go back to the prophet Ezekiel. According to the prophet, the priests who accommodated Israel in her worldliness were still able to remain in their position.

> They are not to come near to serve me as priests or come near any of my holy things or my most holy offerings; they must bear the shame of their detestable practices. Yet I will put them in charge of the duties of the temple and all the work that is to be done in it (Ezek. 44:13–14).

God allowed those who allowed worldliness in the temple of God to stay in the service of the Lord just as He does today with ministers who have no sense of holiness. However, they cannot come close to God. They cannot minister to Him because He is holy and they do not live a separated life. They cannot tell the difference between the holy and the profane. They may, however, be the most active church in town. They may have every program available in their churches. They may feed the hungry, they may stand in protest of the latest social cause, but you couldn't find any sense of holiness in their church because their shepherd is not allowed near God. Churches ultimately reflect the pastor's own relationship with God.

Holiness basically means separation. If there is going to be a sufficient amount of holiness in our churches, there must be a separation between the church and the world. We may be able to attract many people through modern marketing practices but is that all there is to what we are about as a church? Is attendance really a serious issue with God if the only way we can get people into the church is by catering to their fleshly desires? Do we really believe that God would say something like this; "They are not a spiritual people! They are involved in the world in every aspect, but at least they go to church. After all, that's all that is important to me"?

Sheep without a Shepherd

Ezekiel 34:7–10 says:

> Therefore, you shepherds, hear the word of the LORD: As surely as I live, declares the Sovereign LORD, because my flock lacks a shepherd and so has been plundered and has become food for all the wild animals, and because my shepherds did not search for my flock but cared for themselves rather than for my flock, therefore, O shepherds, hear the word of the LORD: This is what the Sovereign LORD says: I am against the shepherds and will hold them accountable for my flock. I will

remove them from tending the flock so that the shepherds can no longer feed themselves. I will rescue my flock from their mouths, and it will no longer be food for them.

Israel was plagued with shepherds that used the flock to meet their own needs. They put their own needs before God's. It appears that God's needs are met through meeting the needs of His sheep. The shepherds should know better. They claim to be spiritually enlightened. Hence they are in the position they are. If they are truly spiritual, they will put their sheep's needs before their own. If they are truly spiritual they will concern themselves with God's will over theirs. Truly spiritual men will put what God wants before the wants of the sheep and recognize that that is the most effective way to meet the needs of His sheep.

"Is the Message Sacred or the Methodology?"

Dean writes: I can hear the argument now! I know what many leaders who have read the preceding comments are thinking. Many pastors have challenged me regarding this same issue whenever I confront the methods they use. Often they will say in effect, "You mistake what we are doing. We aren't compromising the message of the Bible; we're merely updating the means of communication. You are mistaking the methodology for the message." Is that really so? Does God's Word give us total freedom when it comes to methodology?

No, it does not! According to the Word of God the method is just as sacred as the message.

> The LORD your God will cut off before you the nations you are about to invade and dispossess. But when you have driven them out and settled in their land, and after they have been destroyed before you, be careful not to be ensnared by inquiring about their gods, saying, "_How_ do these nations serve their gods? We will do the same." _You must not worship the LORD your God in their way_, because in worshiping their gods, _they do all kinds of detestable things the LORD hates_. They even burn their sons and daughters in the fire as sacrifices to their gods. See that you do all I command you; _do not add to it or take away from it_ (Deut. 12:29–32, emphasis added).

Our culture worships the god of money. We see this all around us everywhere, in everything, including the church. A person concocts all manner of methods and means in order to get what they desire. The general means by which people attract finances are marketing methods. There is nothing wrong with this, so long as the use of marketing is to prosper a business and achieve wealth, with the ultimate goal of furthering the gospel. When we adopt the same means used to achieve worldly wealth in order to promote the worship of God, we have crossed a dangerous line. We have violated God's Word! What is in the world that even comes close to what God offers?

The world and its ways are passing! We see the bondage that people are in, the destruction of the family, the misery and loneliness. All this is caused by the world and its ways! Why would we want to adopt these things? By adding to the Word to make it more acceptable or "significant," by deleting from it to make it more "practical" or easy, we strip it of the very power that enables it to save to the uttermost and deliver completely!

What is so sad is that lost souls around the world are hungering for and running to the true power of the gospel that saves, delivers, and heals, and the church in America is running from it! America's lost souls also want this powerful old-time gospel. They may not know it yet, but it is what they are seeking (see chapter 11, "For the Unbelievers").

We are doing the same thing Jesus accused the Pharisees of in Matthew 15:6–9:

> Thus you *nullify the word of God* for the sake of your tradition. You hypocrites! Isaiah was right when he prophesied about you: "These people honor me with their lips, but their hearts are far from me. They worship me in vain; their teachings are but *rules taught by men*" (emphasis added).

What we fail to realize is that eventually our methodology becomes our message! God gave us in the Second

Commandment the instruction not to make a graven image. It was important to Him that we not try to create a man-made version of symbolizing or explaining Him to the world around us. He was trying to get across an important point: the means by which we communicate God has a dominant influence in the formation of our faith and in our behavior. If it is man-made, the by-product will be man-made "believers." We will be like those mentioned by Jeremiah the prophet.

> My people have committed two sins: They have forsaken me, the spring of living water, and have dug their own cisterns, broken cisterns that cannot hold water (Jer. 2:13).

We have forsaken God the Holy Spirit, the fountain of living water (John 7:38, 39) and have become self-made people who cannot retain what He desires to do by His Spirit in us! There are too many churches filled with people who cannot even retain the most rudimentary truths regarding discipleship. Is it any wonder why Jesus didn't tell His followers to educate themselves with the means of the world used in His day? What did He instruct them to do?

> . . . stay in the city until you have been clothed with power from on high (Luke 24:49).

This clothing of power was not the ability to use worldly means to communicate, but rather was the power to use "other-worldly" means of communication to demonstrate the invisible God's character through acts of supernatural power in the visible world — acts that could never be done by carnal man. Paul summed it up this way:

> My message and my preaching were not with wise and persuasive words, but with a demonstration of the Spirit's power, so that your faith might not rest on men's wisdom, but on God's power (1 Cor. 2:4–5).

Paul knew that this Spirit-filled, Pentecostal form of communication would, in the end, produce people made by and led by God's Spirit. Their faith would not be put in the Church or the clergy or anything of this world. Their faith would rest on the God who raises the dead and has the power to send souls to hell.

Don't you see? God gave us the Bible to reveal himself, and how He wants to be worshiped and followed. We cannot create our own way of worship, our own means of doing His work, even though everywhere in America today we are told to "worship God any way you feel comfortable," and "the methodology isn't sacred. . . ."

This violates God's principles! We cannot worship God in any old way we choose! He gave painstaking detail in the Old Testament in Exodus and Leviticus and throughout the New Testament. He told us that true worshipers would worship in "spirit and in truth." He will not be worshiped any old way! We cannot add to or take away from God's mandated precepts as to how to approach Him.

That's why we are in such need of throwing off the shackles of the world to abandon ourselves once again to His Spirit, allowing Him to build up, cheer up, and edify the Church. God said that He would build His Church, and He does so by His Spirit as men and women of God are completely surrendered to Him and obedient to His every leading and guiding.

We cannot achieve God's ultimate end by man's methodologies! We must turn to God's Spirit for illumination, inspiration, guidance, and power. It was and still is the Holy Spirit's mission to glorify Christ. The less of the Holy Spirit we have in our lives and churches, the less glory is going to Jesus and the more glory is going to man. He is the one that should be filling our minds, our hearts, and our churches! He will administrate the house of worship if we let Him. Only He can truly call and equip. Ultimately, the church derives its authority from the Holy Spirit and not man, because the work of the church is supernatural — it can never and will never be done in the strength of natural man.

I am convinced that this is the clear choice between the two types of priests mentioned in Ezekiel 44. Will we choose to give people what they want — man-made religion powerless to deliver — or what they need — Holy Spirit-breathed religion, like the lame man at the gate called Beautiful?

Endnotes

1. J. Konrad Hölè, *The Worldview Leader* (Issue One, 2005): p. 3–4.

CHAPTER 3

TRUST
AND OBEY

WHERE WOULD JESUS WORSHIP? Would He worship at a church which believes the end justifies the means and subsequently compromises the gospel in order to get people to come?

Ron writes: I believe pragmatism is a problem in the Church today and is creating great (negative) consequences. The philosophy of pragmatism, started by C.S. Pierce and William James, attempts to determine the meaning and truth of all concepts by their practical consequences. William James's book *Pragmatism,* published in 1907, expounds the theory that man knows the true meaning of an idea only when he sees what its effects are.

Pragmatism would say if something doesn't produce the kind of results you are looking for, it is not really truth and

has no meaning. How does this compare to the gospel? The method for spreading the gospel, according to Jesus, would make no sense to the pragmatist. Jesus says if someone slaps you on the cheek, you should let him slap you on the other cheek, also. He says if someone wants your coat, you should give him your shirt also. That's not very pragmatic. That doesn't sound successful at all. A pragmatic view of Christianity would say that it makes good sense to give your life to Jesus because it will result in heaven for you. The problem with that is that it completely ignores the issue of God's glory. Shouldn't a man give his life to Christ because it will ultimately bring glory to God? Heaven is the by-product of salvation; the glory of God is always to be at the forefront of everything we do.

Utilitarianism

Our acceptance of pragmatism has now evolved into utilitarianism. This is a doctrine which determines the worth or value of anything by its utility, suggesting that *the purpose of all action should be to bring about the greatest happiness to the greatest number*. The word "utility" simply means the method of bringing a needed product of service. A "utility vehicle" brings products to people that help them. In our society, we have public utility services such as our electric companies or gas companies. In the utilitarian frame of mind, prayer becomes a utility. It becomes the means to gain the things we want from God. The utilitarian does not pray out of a desire to be with God or even a command to pray. They pray because they have learned of the benefits of prayer.

The utilitarian Christian sees salvation as a utility or as the means of bringing him the greatest amount of joy. His own happiness is his primary motive for being a Christian. Therefore, if he is asked to do something for the Lord that will not necessarily result in his own happiness, he cannot understand its purpose. Subsequently, it becomes very difficult for our pastors today to encourage their people into service. They don't see the personal benefit of it.

The combination of pragmatism and utilitarianism has evolved into a cheap Christianity that would never think of obeying Christ out of principle. Its obedience is based on its own personal comfort and success. For instance, the utilitarian does not pay his tithes out of obedience to the Word of God; he pays them because he has discovered it will profit him. He loves the law of sowing and reaping because of its benefits.

In this frame of mind, the utilitarian's service to the Lord becomes his means of comfort and success. He is involved because of what it means to him, not just because he is commanded to obey God. I once heard a nationally known minister refer to himself as a "blessings" minister because he only deals with the blessings of God. He once said, "If God asks you to do something for Him you have every right to say, 'God, what's in it for me?' " That is the height of utilitarianism. This creates a terrible conflict with the message of the Cross.

> For many walk, of whom I often told you, and now tell you even weeping, that they are enemies of the cross of Christ (Phil. 3:18; NASB).

Is it possible to be a Christian and an enemy of the Cross at the same time? I believe it is, and that many in the American Church would struggle with its message if their pastors seriously dealt with it. What is the message of the Cross? The Cross teaches us that the godly die for the ungodly and that the righteous die for the unrighteous. This is exactly what Jesus did for us on the Cross and this is to be the way of our life if we are going to accomplish anything for the kingdom of God. The message of the Cross is completely contrary to the practice of utilitarianism. How utilitarian is it when you ask God to have mercy on someone who has just slandered you?

PARADIGM SHIFT

There is yet another problem in the Church today called the paradigm shift. First of all, let's look at what a paradigm is. A paradigm is *an overall concept accepted by most people in an intellectual community, because of its effectiveness in explaining a complex process, idea, or set of data.* In other words, a paradigm is the accepted way of doing something because it's what works (the end justifies the means).

For the past few years, the Christian community has been excited about discovering a paradigm shift. In other words, we believe the old "way" of presenting the gospel is outdated and we must adapt the new "way." There has been a shift in what is accepted today. It would seem that the old way of calling sin "sin," is outdated and not very relevant. Today, we must be "spiritually correct" because the world is no longer accepting the old fashioned "hell-fire" type preaching. When was the last time you heard your pastor actually say that God considers a certain activity "sinful"?

Much of what the Church is calling a "seeker-friendly service" should probably be called "sinner-friendly." Sinners can sit in their churches week after week and not realize they are in sin, but at least they feel welcomed.

Some would say, "Ron, you are stuck in a rut. What you are suggesting just doesn't work anymore. Churches that preach hard against sin are not growing." This is where our pragmatism is getting in the way. We have convinced ourselves that "success" (i.e., church growth) is the ultimate goal. Therefore, many feel they can prove me wrong by their "successful" churches.

What do we consider success? Is it obedience to God no matter what, or is it that of reaching our goals no matter what? The pragmatist must neglect total obedience to God because it would rarely produce the kind of immediate results he is looking for. Many of our mega churches are in a dilemma. Suppose God began to deal deeply with the pastor of a large church about changing his message. What would happen to the congregation if he were to go back to the simple gospel and actually preach about Christ rather than just psychology?

I once did a prayer conference for a church in Utah. This particular church had been experiencing a mini revival for some time. They had the habit of having a different guest speaker every Sunday night. The church became known as a revival center. The crowds were coming. Everyone was excited. Things were happening. With time, God began to deal with the pastor about actually shepherding his flock. He told him to do away with the special services and simply go back to preaching a simple gospel. The pastor struggled with this for quite some time. Finally, he did what God asked him to do. When I got there to do the conference there were only 80 people in church. I asked him what had happened. He said, "Once I went back to pastoring them and correcting their lives, we lost several hundred people." Here is the dilemma. We have many pastors who have built their churches on a "feel good gospel." If they were to actually change over to the simple gospel, they would lose too many to continue to pay the bills of the church.

I CHANGE NOT

For I, the LORD, do not change . . . (Mal. 3:6).

If God really meant that He doesn't change, then what about us when we do change? God is telling us that He doesn't have paradigm shifts. The very things He established in the beginning are still in place. The Ten Commandments are as valid today as they were when Moses received them.

Since there has been a paradigm shift concerning the status and acceptance of divorce, pastors can no longer preach against it. If a pastor took a strong public stance against divorce, he would not be popular, and his church would not be considered a "cutting-edge" church. To be relevant today, a pastor must focus only on the happiness one can experience after remarriage, while one marriage after another goes down the tubes in his happy, relevant, pragmatic church.

Though we have shifted away from honoring the Ten Commandments in order to remain relevant, happy, and successful, the Commandments still stand. Do you suppose God was serious when he said, "You shall not commit adultery," or, "You shall not covet your neighbor's wife"? These things often precede divorce, and if our sheep do not hear this message they tend to go their own way.

ISAIAH

What would have happened to the prophet Isaiah if he had had our success mentality? Consider God's words to the prophet in chapter 6 of his book:

> And He said, "Go, and tell this people: 'Keep on listening, but do not perceive; keep on looking, but do not understand. Render the hearts of this people insensitive, their ears dull, and their eyes

dim, lest they see with their eyes, hear with their ears, understand with their hearts, and return and be healed' " (Isa. 6:9–10; NASB).

If Isaiah had our attitude today, he would certainly have complained, "Lord, that is not a formula for success. I don't believe making the people insensitive is going to bring me all the acclaim I am looking for as a prophet of God. Insensitivity is not 'spiritually correct.' Don't you understand that there has been a paradigm shift?"

What about Peter? When Jesus was talking to him in John 21, He predicted his death as a martyr.

> Truly, truly, I say to you, when you were younger, you used to gird yourself, and walk wherever you wished; but when you grow old, you will stretch out your hands, and someone else will gird you, and bring you where you do not wish to go (John 21:18; NASB).

Jesus began by pointing out that initially Peter was a pragmatist but that He was going to change him. He said, in essence, "When you were young, you did what made sense to you. But when you become old, you will do what makes sense to me." That which makes sense to God may differ greatly from what makes sense to us. We must keep in mind that this is not a matter of success, it's a matter of obedience.

It's hard to imagine Peter saying, "But, Lord, if I die as a martyr I will look like a failure. I will look weak. I will look like I am at the mercy of the ungodly." Then as the realization of what he is saying hits him, he turns his tear-filled eyes to his Savior and says, "I will look like you."

In our pragmatic day, we face a great challenge. Can we simply obey God? Can we simply do the right thing, especially when it doesn't appear successful? What if changing our current "feel good" message to the message of the Cross caused our churches to decrease in size? Could we obey then? What if God understands something about obedience to Him that we don't yet understand?

OBEDIENCE NO MATTER WHAT!

Does this mean that churches shouldn't grow? Not at all! Don't you think that God wants the Church to grow? Don't you believe that He is interested in the souls of those in your community? This, however, is not a matter of church growth. I am talking about philosophy of ministry; I'm talking about obeying God no matter what.

> Or does not the potter have a right over the clay, to make from the same lump one vessel for honorable use, and another for common use? (Rom. 9:21; NASB).

God has the right to use us in any way He pleases. I have been in many large churches that have a great sense of the presence of God and some large churches that haven't had any presence in a long time. I have also been in some small churches where the presence of God would bowl you over and some small churches that have such a religious spirit that God is nowhere to be found. This is not about size of the church; it's about our twisted definition of success.

What if you are one of those vessels that God has designed for common use? Can the clay tell the potter what to make out of it? What if nothing you do will be looked upon as successful from the rest of the church world? Could you be content with a simple obedience to God then? Obedience seems so much easier when it results in what the world calls success, but success is not determined by the world's standards. Success is complete obedience to God.

WHAT ABOUT HIM?

After Jesus told Peter that he was going to die as a martyr, He implied that John was going to live a wonderful full life.

> Peter, turning around, saw the disciple whom Jesus loved following them; the one who also had leaned back on His breast at the supper, and . . . said to Jesus, "Lord, and what about this man?" Jesus said to him, "If I want him to remain until I come, what is that to you? You follow Me!" (John 21:20–22; NASB).

Peter was struggling with the pragmatism of dying as a martyr; it certainly wouldn't be utilitarian. Then he asked Jesus about John.

He said essentially, "If I have to die this way, what about John?"

Jesus responds, in essence, by saying, "What do My dealings with John have to do with your obedience to Me? If I want John to live forever without any suffering whatsoever, what does that have to do with your obedience to Me? I have asked one thing of you and one thing only; follow Me."

How could Peter live in our current world of pragmatic/utilitarian goals of success and happiness knowing that he was going to die as a martyr? If it were not for the possibility of greatness, many men would not even be in the ministry today.

SUCCESSFUL FAILURES

Would you believe me if I told you the Bible defines certain failures as great men of faith?

They were stoned, they were sawn in two, they were tempted, they were put to death with the sword; they went about in sheepskins, in goatskins, being destitute, afflicted, ill-treated (men of whom the world was not worthy), wandering in deserts and mountains and caves and holes in the ground. And all these, having gained approval through their faith, did not receive what was promised (Heb. 11:37–39; NASB).

Pragmatism attempts to determine the meaning and truth of our actions by the practical consequences we are able to perceive with our natural senses. How practical does death seem to the one who has a mindset of pragmatism? The Bible says these men were great men of faith and that they gained the approval of God even though they did not receive the thing they were seeking. These men were successful failures. How could that be? How could those who failed in their mission ever be considered a success? The answer to that is found in God's definition of success. Success is total obedience to God no matter what.

THE APOSTATE CHURCH

The end result of our pragmatism, utilitarianism, and paradigm shifting is an apostate church. Second Timothy 3 describes the apostate church. It will be ruled by men who are in love with self (utilitarian), men who will be lovers of money (pragmatism), and men without self-control (paradigm shifting), (see 2 Tim. 3:2–3). He then contrasted that with obedience to God no matter what by talking about suffering for Christ (see 2 Tim. 3:11).

The apostate believer marks the apostate church. The apostate believer is a man who can never come to the knowledge of the truth though he is ever learning (see 2 Tim. 3:7). He is a man who can hear truth over and over but never allow what he knows to prompt him into any service for God. It will be a day of high-speed boats and backyard cookouts, but no service to God. Service to God (dying to self) would not be pragmatic.

What's the bottom line to all of this? I think the answer can be found in the Word of God.

> How blessed is the man who does not walk in the counsel of the wicked, nor stand in the path of sinners, nor sit in the seat of scoffers! But his delight is in the law of the LORD, and in His law he meditates day and night (Ps. 1:1–2; NASB).

We must stop allowing the world's definition of success (counsel of the ungodly) be our guide. Our delight must be in the law of God. That is to be our meditation! That is to be our guide!

CHAPTER 4

THE "GOD-CHURCH" VERSUS
THE "GOOD-CHURCH"

WHERE WOULD JESUS WORSHIP? Would Jesus attend a church which has good worship, good preaching, and even good fellowship but very little of His presence, no repentance, and very few growing spiritually?

Ron writes: When Satan deceived Adam and Eve, he did so by appealing to man's good side rather than his evil side. Satan deceived us into thinking that man will become like God. He said to Eve, "For God knows that in the day you eat from it your eyes will be opened, and you will be like God, knowing good and evil" (Gen. 3:5; NASB).

Interestingly enough, man's problem is not that he understands "evil," but rather that he understands "good." Our "goodness" is what tends to keep us from God rather than evil. It is relatively easy to get an evil man to admit his

need for God. It is much more difficult to get a good man to admit his need for God. Our goodness makes us believe we are like God. We know that God is good, so when we are good we believe we are like Him. Subsequently, our goodness tends to keep us from repentance. We believe our goodness will get us to heaven. This has been the great debate between Christians and non-Christians down through the ages.

THE GOOD CHURCH

That debate has now entered the arena of the church world. One of the spiritual problems in our country today comes from the struggle between the "good church" and the "God church." Today we have many good churches. They have good worship. They have good preaching. Everything about them is good, but very little about them is God.

We know how to be good. We learned that when we fell from innocence. Typically, Christians are good people. Therefore, the problem is not in goodness itself, but rather in thinking that goodness is the same as God-ness. We can be very good people and worldly at the same time. I know many "good people" who spend a lot of money on worldly entertainment. Their goodness causes them to seek out a good church. They can attend a good church without feeling any sense of conviction, because most good churches lack a convicting presence of God.

On any given Saturday night, many "good church people" can be found intertwined with the world. To have watched them go about the evening you would not have been able to tell them from those that had no sense of God at all. Much to their relief, they find that on Sunday they can go to their good church and enjoy some of the most talented musicians in town, lift their hands in worship, listen to the most polished sermon they have ever heard, and come away feeling good about themselves.

I once heard the testimony of a woman who was part of a revival in Canada a few years ago. She was talking about how she ended up in her church on a Saturday night rather than at the bars. She was being interviewed on radio at the revival site when she said to the man interviewing her, "I don't usually come to church dressed in a slinky black evening gown. I was dressed to go out dancing at the bars, as I usually do on Saturday nights, when I happened to drive by my church and decided to come in."

What I found completely fascinating was her lack of connection between her regular activities and her commitment to God. I believe this is a great problem in today's church. We seem to lack the ability to cause people to associate their "life outside of church," to their "life inside of church." This lady was a regular attendee of this church and never did think the issue of her going out dancing every Saturday night in the bars in slinky black dresses was in conflict with her church. She had no sense of holiness.

When you think about it, why should she make the connection between her sin and the lack of sensing God in her life? She attends one of those "good churches." Every week she sits in her pew and never hears anything about turning away from the world and all of its ungodly attractions. She hasn't made the connection that worldliness and holiness are two separate worlds. When she goes to her church she absorbs the wonderful worship music, she donates her time to worthy causes because she is a good person, while at the same time she would be hard pressed find the presence of God in her life.

Our own goodness has become the most dangerous thing about us. The good church, the seeker-sensitive church, the church that chooses to make everyone but Jesus feel comfortable, is the most deceptive church in town. Though they seem friendly and "spiritually correct," they keep people in their sin. In actuality, the "good church" is a most deceitful church.

Dean writes: I have always felt that holiness is a Pentecostal issue. It is probably related to my initial discipleship, but it is, after all, founded in the Scriptures.

> When he comes, he will convict the world of guilt in regard to sin and righteousness and judgment (John 16:8).

As those people who have been filled with the Spirit, who say we want His moving, we must embrace the fact that where the Holy Spirit moves, He will bring people some pretty uncomfortable thoughts and feelings. This is exactly the opposite of modern trends in the American church where we seek more than ever the comfort of people first and biblical truth second. We seem to want people happy, not holy!

My wife and I met a wonderful young woman who by her own testimonial is a Christian. She and her husband went to a good, well-respected Bible college; they attend a fine modern church, which uses up-to-date church growth principles and is seeing a steady increase in attendance. She and her husband are involved and committed.

But herein lies the dilemma. She is very popular with her fellow workers in that she goes to bars with them for beer and margaritas. She never misses a chance. The problem is, she is sure of the call of God on her and her husband's lives to be pastors and yet sees no conflict between her behavior and the call of God on her life.

What is at issue here is a generation that is coming up through the Church that is being raised in the absence of the convicting power of the Holy Spirit. We are teaching more steps to better living, but the precepts of the Word of God are largely ignored. When we do teach on righteousness and holiness, we do so without offering the power Jesus said we would need to BE a witness through a God-fearing lifestyle.

There is more great teaching on marriage in the church in America than ever before, but more divorces. There is more great teaching and cell groups on freedom from your problems, but more bondage in believers. We have substituted man's wisdom and methods for the presence and power of the living God!

Transformation never happens through preaching and teaching. They are vehicles toward change. True change happens when a person's stubborn will meets with God's Spirit at an altar of prayer and surrenders in total exhaustion!

Look at the Upper Room. Those scared and, in some cases, Christ-denying apostles were completely changed when they prayed for all those days and finally clothed themselves with the Holy Spirit as He also clothed himself with them. Their cowardice turned into courage, their carnality into sacrifice, and their selfishness into love. That is what this generation in America is looking for!

THE GOD CHURCH

Ron writes: The God church, the church that calls sin "sin," is looked down upon today by most other churches. It is not a "spiritually correct" church. If it catches you doing something wrong it will say, "*Repent!*" If you persist in your sin it may even "put you out of the church" so that on the Day of the Lord your soul might be saved. Initially, this seems harsh and un-caring, when in reality it is the most caring church in town. The church that causes you to feel "God" rather than just "good" is the church closest to God.

The good church cannot offer you God. It can only affirm you in your own goodness. It can make you feel like God, because it makes you feel good and that makes us feel like God. The problem is — we are not good. The Bible says no one is good except God. So eventually our own goodness will run out and in a time of need we will have nothing, and we will know that we have nothing. Do you know what we will do then? We will seek a God church.

A minister from a mainline church recalled in a magazine article how his church had tried to help a spiritually needy family. The father — an abusive husband — had thrust his home into turmoil. The church staff took his children to camp and a women's group reached out to the man's wife in efforts to restore the family, but nothing seemed to work.

Months later, the minister saw the man on the street. His countenance had radically changed. Bubbling with excitement, the former rabble-rouser described attending a Pentecostal church. "It's wonderful," the man enthused. "I've been saved and received the gift of the Spirit."

"I can tell," nodded the minister. "You look totally different."

"I am," the man said.

The preacher responded, "I'm sorry our church couldn't help you."

"Preacher, you were offering aspirin, and I needed chemotherapy," said the man.

In light of the preceding account let's consider these startling facts; the Episcopal Church, the United Methodist Church, and the United Church of Christ have asked the

Supreme Court to rule against the Boy Scouts of America because they won't allow homosexuals to be scoutmasters.

John Shelby Spong, former bishop of the Episcopal Church wrote in a book, *Why Christianity Must Change or Die*, "We were not created in God's image in any literal way. We simply evolved out of lower forms of life and ultimately developed a higher consciousness. We human beings do not live in sin. We are not born in sin. We do not need to have the stain of our original sin washed away in baptism. We are not fallen creatures. We have rather emerged out of our evolutionary past, and we are still being formed."

According to Drew University theology professor Thomas Oden, the whole mainline seminary culture is losing the faith. Oden wrote, "If you doubt the accuracy of what I have stated, ask any recent graduate of a liberal seminary if they know of anyone who still defiantly holds on to belief in the incarnation and Resurrection."

How did such outlandish non-Christian views take hold among Christians? It is believed they changed because their seminaries eventually changed over to liberal perspectives embracing the popular thought of relevance, which became popular in the 1960s. Relevance implies *a close logical relationship with, and importance to, the matter under consideration.* In other words, when the Church loses its power and influence through its own lack of personal prayer and holiness, it historically has shifted over to believing that the only way to be effective is to present the gospel in a way that will seem current and up-to-date. Do you see what relevance is? It's man trying to do, through his own logic, what seems good to him — what only the power of the gospel can do. Relevance is an effort to appear not so out of it. Subsequently, we have churches that once were full of life holding on to doctrines of devils today.

Some of you may be saying that all the statistics I have been quoting have to do with mainline churches — and why should we expect anything more from churches that don't really know Christ personally, anyway? My point is this: that may be who those churches are today, but they started out as fiery churches that were blazing for God. Eventually, they changed. Today, we are not dealing exclusively with just mainline churches, but rather evangelical churches (many of them Pentecostal) that are beginning to sway in their theology in order to be relevant to today's society.

GOD CANNOT BE THWARTED!

I have a good friend in the ministry who has a slightly different philosophy of ministry than I do. He once told his congregation, "I don't shear my sheep." My problem with that is that sheep need shearing from time to time. Shearing the sheep in this context is that of calling sin, "sin." I will come back to this thought in the next few pages, but first we must look at the idea of being thwarted.

> For the LORD Almighty has purposed, and who
> can thwart him? (Isa. 14:27).

Who can thwart God? God has purposed, and nothing can thwart Him. I suppose for this word to mean much to us we need to look into its meaning. The Hebrew word for "thwart" is *parar,* which means to break up or divide. God has purposed and nothing will divide that purpose or break up that purpose.

Now lets consider Hebrews 12:1:

> Therefore, since we are surrounded by such a great cloud of witnesses, let us throw off everything that hinders and the sin that so easily entangles, and let us run with perseverance the race marked out for us.

The cloud of witnesses refers to all the giants of the faith that we read about in Hebrews 11. Most of the theologians on this subject believe it is simply referring to the witness they were to the faith, and that now that they have gone on before us, we should continue to look to them as an encouragement to continue ourselves. It's not saying that they are actually watching us from heaven — but rather that we should follow their testimony and witness.

Those who died in the faith did so because they stayed the course. Paul the Apostle often used the *race* as an analogy of our pursuit of heaven. We are all to be on a continual path toward God. Did you know that the only thing that moves toward God is the Church? The world is at a standstill in regard to spiritual progression. The Church is to always be striving toward God. Paul refers to it as being in a race. And the one who stays on the racetrack or stays with the simple gospel message wins.

The writer of Hebrews does the same type of thing here. He says, in essence, "Since this is the most important race of your life — throw off everything that hinders."

The word "hinders" is the Greek word, *ogkos*, which means a mass, a burden, or something bulging because of its load. We are to throw off everything that hinders and the sin that so easily entangles. The word *entangles* also means to thwart. It is the Greek word *euperistatos*, which means to dart in every direction (thwart). Therefore, our understanding of this verse is that we are on a race track trying to run a race, while sin, this heavy burden, tries to get us to go off course.

> They will be entangled among thorns and drunk
> from their wine; they will be consumed like dry
> stubble (Nah. 1:10).

Here is the picture the Bible paints for us. We are to walk the straight and narrow road. The reason for this is because the road is lined with thorn bushes. However, our attraction to this old world means we have gotten away from the straight and narrow way and our own sin has forced us to the sides of the road (we stagger under the weight of sin) where we get entangled in the thorn bushes. To be entangled means to no longer progress toward God. Remember, it is only the Church that is progressing toward God — the world is not in pursuit of God. The world will keep you from moving toward God. Have you ever heard of a worldly person moving closer to God?

This is the purpose of shearing sheep. A sheep's long wool spiritually represents the growing trend we all have toward carnality. If it isn't trimmed from time to time, it gets so wooly that if you even get close to the side of the road you will get caught by the thorn bushes. This is, in part, why the good church is the most deceptive church there is. They preach a message that makes it easy for the sheep to get caught up in the spirit of this world, thus no longer truly progressing toward God. The God church will shear the sheep out of a love for them and their spiritual progress.

CHAPTER 5

CORE
VALUES

WHERE WOULD JESUS WORSHIP? Would Jesus
worship in a church that has no strong convictions and fell
for every new fad that came along, desperately seeking for
the key to success?

Ron writes: For 20 years I traveled full-time teaching conferences literally around the world. I have been in
thousands of churches of every type and make up. If there
is one thing I have observed during this time it is the lack
of good solid theology coming from the pastor's heart.
The preaching that is coming from most of our pulpits
fits into the category of psychology rather than theology.
There is a lot of feel-good-ism being preached today. If our
shepherds do not know exactly what they believe, then
they will believe whatever seems to be working at the time.

This is what I consider the greatest problem the Pentecostal church faces.

If there was ever a need for the Word of God to go forth from our pulpits with all the power of God behind it, it's now. It is very difficult to find ministers who have a strong theology, and their treatment of the Word of God proves that. I was talking to a minister friend of mine who shared with me how when he was an associate pastor he heard his senior pastor preach from the same verse three different times, each time taking a different view of the same verse. If Christianity is weak in America it's because we have so many preachers who do not know what they believe and subsequently cannot say it straight.

When I planted Prayer House in 1999, one of the requirements for us was to attend a boot camp for church planters. I found this experience to be most beneficial, especially in the area of defining core values. A core value is defined as something you would be willing to die for. Core values are really a reflection of a person's theology. If a person does not know what they believe, if they are not rock solid on their theology, it is impossible for them to have core values. It's from the lack of core values in a person's life, and specifically a pastor's life, that they can be tossed to and fro, carried about by every wind of doctrine. If a pastor lacks core values then he becomes subject to every new fad, every new book, and every new thing under the sun, to try to get his church to grow. Their churches will be continually redefining themselves.

No Vision, No Restraint

> Where there is no revelation, the people cast off restraint (Prov. 29:18).

Many of us remember this verse from the King James Version, which says, "Where there is no vision, the people perish." In either case, the whole idea of the verse is that sheep need to be led and if the shepherd has no vision, no revelation, his sheep will show no restraint. A vision is a discipline. Yes, it may start off as a spiritual experience like when God took Abram outside to look at the stars in the heavens and told him that his descendants would outnumber them. However, that vision became the guiding factor of his life. When a man of God has a revelation of where God is leading His Church, that revelation restrains him. It causes him to live a certain way. Subsequently, he will preach passionately toward his vision. He will lead his sheep through his passion.

Vision, or revelation, primarily comes through theology. We cannot gain a sense of what God is saying and doing if we do not know what we believe. Have you ever noticed that leaders rarely attend leadership conferences? Do you think Zig Ziglar ever attends a John Maxwell seminar? If he ever showed up it would be as a co-speaker, never as an attendee, because men of vision don't need to follow another man's vision. Leaders lead from a point of passion. They are not so interested in what others are saying because they have a burning message in their own hearts. They know what God is saying to them and they won't be deterred from that vision. The biggest moneymaking enterprise in the church today is leadership conferences. Pastors are spending millions of dollars on books to help them lead when in reality, through the folded hand and an open Bible, God can do great things. God can save you a lot of money.

We must keep in mind that core values are nouns. The way we achieve them is through a certain action, or verb. One of our core values is souls. Souls must be at the forefront of every church's values. Keep in mind, the value is souls. How you achieve your goal is where churches can vary. Evangelism is the verb attached to the value here. Evangelism is what we do — souls are what we value. We cannot value evangelism because then we would make it sacred. There is nothing sacred about walking door to door to share the gospel. There is something quite sacred about the souls behind the door.

I had an interesting experience during my boot camp. We were in the middle of a workshop on values. The leader asked us to list our values on a paper and then we would discuss them. So my wife and I were talking about what our values are. I listed prayer as the first value. When one of the leaders came walking by my table he looked at my first value and said, "You put prayer down as something you value?"

I said, "Yes," feeling quite spiritual.

He then said, "I wouldn't put that down as one of my values."

I thought to myself, *Well, as soon as you are as spiritual as I am, you will.*

He continued, "Anybody can pray, Buddhists pray, Hindus pray, Muslims pray. Is all you value the ability to pray?"

At that point I was quite confused. Finally he asked, "Why do you pray?"

I thought for a minute and said, "I really love the intimacy with God that comes through prayer."

"There's your core value," he responded. "You value intimacy with God; that's the core value. Prayer is merely the means to attaining the value."

I realized that I was putting a value on the verb, the action. We cannot do that because we tend to make anything we practice sacred. Prayer is not sacred. The presence of God is, intimacy with Him is. I have been in hundreds of churches that emphasize prayer because they think God loves it when we pray. Subsequently, they are promoting something they rarely practice.

The Bible talks about core values in the Book of Ephesians.

> . . . built on the foundation of the apostles and prophets, with Christ Jesus himself as the chief cornerstone. In him the whole building is joined

together and rises to become a holy temple in the Lord (Eph. 2:20–21).

"The foundation of the apostles and prophets with Jesus as the Cornerstone," could very well be called "core values." The whole New Testament church was built on a set of values, and many of those values cost the believers their lives.

It's very difficult today to build the church on values because we are a valueless society. Conviction is not a strong suit of the church today. That is precisely why our pastors must be.

One report about that which draws people to a church today said that there are three things people are looking for when they visit a church. The first thing is **ease of parking**. What is the parking lot like — how far do we have to walk? Secondly, it's the **comfort of the seating**. Is it soft and cushy? The third thing is the **worship style**. I can understand the worship aspect of a church service being important, but what struck me was there was no mention at all of the preached Word of God, of discipleship, or even fellowship as part of what people consider important in a church. The fastest-growing churches in our nation today preach very little conviction. They make sure all of our creature comforts are taken care of as their first priority.

I don't want church to be physically uncomfortable. That's why we spent thousands of dollars on the chairs in our sanctuary. It may not be wrong to be physically comfortable, but it is wrong to be spiritually comfortable. I believe, as disciples of Christ, we should always be looking for ways to be challenged in our faith. If we get to thinking that the church exists to meet our physical needs then we will lose sight of our whole mission on earth. You cannot fulfill the great commission and be self-centered at the same time.

I once watched Pastor Joel Osteen being interviewed on TV by Larry King. He pastors the largest church in America in Houston, Texas. They can seat 16,000 in their church and they have three services every Sunday. When he was asked if he preached on the issue of sin he said, "No I don't. People know they are sinners, they don't need me to tell them." I take exception to that. I had to be convinced that I was a sinner. When I first heard the gospel I had a hard time with it because I figured I would be going to heaven based on my own goodness. People don't know they are sinners, especially when they go to a church that continually affirms them and strokes them.

We will never be drawn to a life of holiness and purity and prayer when we listen to preachers who never deal with it. Feel-good-ism is only acceptable when you have no core values. Feel-good-ism is counter-productive to self-denial.

I'm not comfortable in my relationship with Christ. I always want more of Jesus — and I want my church to want the same. The only way to get more and more of Him is to die more and more to self. And the only way to be able to die to self on a consistent basis is to have conviction in your life.

Conviction is another way of saying *core values*. Core values are the things in your life that you would be willing to give your life for, in the same way the early Apostles did. Almost all of Jesus' original 12 disciples died as martyrs, not being willing to give up on their core values.

I'm going to share what I believe to be the five core values of a Jesus-sensitive church. You may have additional values in your church but these five are a must. They are:

1. Intimacy with God
2. A knowledge of God
3. The glory of God
4. Relationships
5. Souls

All of our core values tie into our mission statement, which is: "Connecting with our God, our neighbors, and our world!"

The first part of our mission statement is "Connecting with our God." The core values that fit here are: **Intimacy with God.** In order to truly connect with God there must be an intimacy between you and Him. The verb here is *prayer.* The next core value that fits under this category is **A knowledge of God.** We must also have knowledge of God if we are going to connect with Him. The verb here is the *study* of His Word. The third value is **The Glory of God.** If we are going to bring glory to Him, we must *worship* Him.

The second part of our mission statement is "Connecting with our neighbors," which is accomplished through the value we put on Relationships. This is where our small group ministry comes in. There are very few things that take place in our church that equal the value of small groups in terms of relationships.

The third part of our mission statement is "Connecting with our world," which is accomplished through the value we put on souls. The only way to connect with our world is to win them to Christ. The verbs attached to this value are *evangelism* and *missions*.

I trust you can see how all of these things are intertwined. Our mission statement, our vision statement, and our core values all tie together to make up the heart of our church. This is what we stand for as a church. I want my people to understand these things so that they can explain them to others who may ask about our church. Rather than just saying, "Come to our church. It's such a nice church," I want them to be able to say, "Our mission statement is, *connecting with our God, our neighbors, and our world.*" I want them to be able to explain what our core values are. If they cannot tell them that our church has a strong emphasis on intimacy with God, on the Word of God, on the glory of God, on souls, and on relationships — what will they tell them? Are they just going to tell them that we have a nice new building, and usually we keep the grass mowed?

Church Is Not about Church

Did you know that Jesus never intended for church to be what we have made it? We never should have become an organization that is all about us. When we get to heaven one day Jesus is not going to sit us down and say, "Tell me all about your church. How big did it get, did you keep it clean, were the pews comfortable, what about the holidays, did you have some good Christmas plays and Easter pageants?"

This is why I'm greatly concerned about that which has become the deciding factor about how to pick a church today. If it is decided upon the carnal comforts it offers then our whole mentality has shifted over to believing that church is really about church, rather than souls. Wouldn't you rather be able to sit down with Jesus one day in heaven and say, "Lord, we won many, many, souls to Your kingdom. We discipled thousands. You didn't die in vain. We spent our whole life as a witness to who You are."

CHAPTER 6

WHO SPEAKS FOR GOD?

WHERE WOULD JESUS WORSHIP? Would Jesus feel comfortable worshiping in a church where the pastor's ego is bigger than his love for the Lord?

Ron writes: I had just finished a discussion with one of our ministry's advisors when a statement he had made struck me. We were talking about some of the current events taking place in the Church when he said, "Who speaks for God?"

I said, "What do you mean?"

He continued, "Doesn't it seem that everybody claims to speak for God?"

He then asked, "Don't you claim to speak for God when you teach?" I hadn't really given that a lot of thought until that time. He finished by saying, "I claim that what I say is, in essence, speaking for God."

WHERE
WOULD
JESUS
WORSHIP?

It's possible that this is a much bigger issue than most people think. It seems everybody wants to be the "voice of God" on earth. However, the issue is not so much "speaking for God," because everyone bringing God's Word is, in essence, "speaking for Him." The issue is more about the desire to be seen as the one God speaks through. Why is it everyone would like to be the "one"? I believe it comes from a root of pride. If we can prove that God speaks through us, then we can prove that we are close to God. One may ask, "Is it wrong to want to be close to God?" Obviously not! However, if a person wants people to think he is close to God for the purpose of personal gain or controlling others, he has a wrong spirit.

In 2 Peter 1:21, we read:

> For no prophecy was ever made by an act of human will, but men moved by the Holy Spirit spoke from God (NAS95).

If we were to Americanize this verse it may sound something like; "No *true* prophecy was ever made by an act of human will." There have been an abundance of "prophecies" made by the human will, but they really have nothing to do with God. It's clear from Scripture that men who are moved by the Holy Spirit can speak for God. To be moved by the Spirit of God, one must have pure motives. Simeon was a man that was moved by the Spirit of God. We read of him in Luke 2:25:

And behold, there was a man in Jerusalem whose name was Simeon; and this man was righteous and devout, looking for the consolation of Israel; and the Holy Spirit was upon him (NASB).

Simeon had pure motives. He was righteous and just. Subsequently, the Spirit of God could use him. When Simeon was moved to go to the temple, he saw the baby Jesus there and instantly knew that this child was the Messiah. How many other people brushed up against the baby as His parents were taking Him through the crowd to get to the temple without ever realizing that the child they just touched was the Messiah? Because Simeon was "moved by the Spirit of God," he had an insight others did not have.

When a person speaks from insight given him because of uprightness, he speaks for God. When a person speaks just from knowledge about God, he speaks about the things of God, but might not necessarily be speaking the things God would have him speak at that particular time. He may be a voice for God, but not necessarily the voice of God for that very moment.

MOSES AND AARON

In the Book of Exodus, God calls Moses to free the Children of Israel from their bondage in Egypt. However, Moses does not believe he is able to speak to the people. We read of this in Exodus 4:10:

Then Moses said to the LORD, "Please, Lord, I have never been eloquent, neither recently nor in time past, nor since Thou hast spoken to Thy servant; for I am slow of speech and slow of tongue" (NASB).

God was not impressed with the lack of understanding Moses had. He challenges Moses by stating that He is the one that made the mouth of men. He made the speaking, the deaf, the dumb, and the blind. He can certainly make Moses able to speak. But Moses continues to lack faith. In Exodus 4:14 (NASB), God decides to use Aaron as His mouthpiece:

Then the anger of the LORD burned against Moses, and He said, "Is there not your brother Aaron the Levite? I know that he speaks fluently. . . ."

Then in the next verse we read:

And you are to speak to him and put the words in his mouth; and I, even I, will be with your mouth and his mouth, and I will teach you what you are to do.

In the next verse we discover that Moses does not do the actual speaking but rather Aaron. Moses seems to remain physically silent throughout the whole ordeal.

Moreover, he shall speak for you to the people; and it shall come about that he shall be as a mouth for you, and you shall be as God to him.

Here we begin to see Moses as a type of Christ and Aaron as a minister/prophet. Moses is as God to him. Moses is not actually Aaron's god; he is as God to him. Moses speaks to Aaron and Aaron brings the message. Aaron becomes the voice of God to Pharaoh. As we read about Moses and Aaron attempting to free the Hebrew children from Pharaoh's grip we see that Moses was not doing the speaking. Moses was silent in Pharaoh's presence; Aaron did the speaking. Aaron is the voice but the attention is not on Aaron, it's on Moses.

We don't read about Aaron as the great deliverer of God's people. We don't read about the great faith of Aaron. Aaron is merely a mouthpiece — Moses is the deliverer! Moses is the leader! Moses is the one with the direct line to God! Yet Moses is physically silent. However, because Aaron spoke what Moses told him to speak and did not speak of his own, the people developed a great respect for Moses. In Exodus 11:3 we read:

> Furthermore, the man Moses himself was greatly esteemed in the land of Egypt, both in the sight of Pharaoh's servants and in the sight of the people (NASB).

Aaron is "the voice," but gets none of the attention. It was never God's intention for Aaron to get the attention. It was God's intention to establish Moses as the voice of God for the Hebrew children. If Aaron had had an ego like most of us, Moses might never have been established as the one worthy to lead.

Our clamoring for greatness has greatly damaged the leadership of Jesus. Not only does the world not hold Jesus in great esteem, neither does the Church. It is very difficult to get the Church to live according to the Word of God because the church lacks a sufficient example of humility in its pastors. Not only do we want to be "the voice," we also want to be the ones that get the glory.

JOHN THE BAPTIST

Isaiah, the prince of the Old Testament prophets, foretold of the ministry of John the Baptist 700 years before his day. In Isaiah 40:3, we read:

> A voice is calling, "Clear the way for the LORD in the wilderness; make smooth in the desert a highway for our God" (NASB).

John the Baptist spoke for God. He was the man of the hour. He had God's message for the people of his day.

Why would any of us struggle with gaining the right to speak for God? I believe it is from the separation that would be required to speak for God! We don't like separation. However, revelation requires separation, and without revelation, we do not speak for God. The revelation of divine healing comes through being separated from health. The revelation of God as our provider comes through being separated from abundance, which is what giving is all about. Separation develops humility. Without humility we cannot see God.

John the Baptist saw things that others did not see. He proved the motive of his heart in his willingness to live a life separated from his peers. It would be no small thing to live in the desert away from the crowds, away from the activity of the market place. Not only was John's separation physical, it was also a separation from the current thought or philosophies of the day. Subsequently, when he came on the scene and re-entered the "real" world, he instantly saw God's message. He preached repentance to his own peers.

He said, in essence, "There is no way you are ready for the appearing of the Messiah. You must repent." Nothing has really changed, has it? Those who separate themselves, those who spend time in the closet of prayer, come out from it and can easily "see" the message. They look at a carnal church and say, in essence, "There is no way you are ready for the soon return of the Messiah."

Consider this: God is spirit, but we are flesh and blood. If we are going to gain His voice, we must first see Him. If we are going to see Him, we must be set apart from this world. This is more of a separation of philosophies than anything else. The philosophy of this world is the exaltation of man. Everything this world does is an effort to exalt man over God. To die to that philosophy is the initial start of separation.

A person must die to the desire to be THE voice. How can a man who wants to be perceived as spiritual actually have a message that exalts God? His own desire to be seen as spiritual exalts him above God and ruins the message even if it's right. Don't confuse the desire to be seen as spiritual with true spirituality. I believe all men should pursue true spirituality. What I am talking about is a driving desire to be perceived as spiritual by other men. This was the problem with the Pharisees.

I once counseled a man concerning his marriage. His wife wanted a divorce; he did not. One of the struggles this man was facing was that his wife was getting council from some of the members of her church encouraging her to go ahead with the divorce. Certain "successful" divorcees were telling her it really was possible for her to make it on her own. Whether these "counselors" had made it in the world or not is not the point. The point is they were giving advice that is contrary to the Word of God. They were exalting themselves above God. They were saying their way is better than God's way. Do they speak for God? They may think they do because of their perceived success, but if they are contradicting God's Word, they don't.

Rejoicing in His Voice

John the Baptist's words were anointed. He spoke for God. He was "the voice," and yet when Jesus came on the scene, John's greatest thrill was to give up his voice so that the voice of the Lamb of God could be heard.

In the third chapter of John, we read an account where John's disciples came to him wondering whether or not

Jesus was really the Messiah. John responded to them in John 3:28–30 saying:

> You yourselves bear me witness, that I said, "I am not the Christ," but, "I have been sent before Him." He who has the bride is the bridegroom; but the friend of the bridegroom, who stands and hears him, rejoices greatly because of the bridegroom's voice. And so this joy of mine has been made full. He must increase, but I must decrease (NASB).

John had sacrificed in the desert. He lived on a diet of locusts and honey. He lived apart from the crowds. Very few people even knew he was out in the desert. Those who did see him probably thought he was a crazy man. Finally, John got his day. It was time to start preaching, because the Lamb of God's time had come. Suddenly, this hermit had center stage. He developed a group of disciples. Though he was preaching a hard message of repentance, the crowds still came out to hear him. He was baptizing them one after another.

Just about the time his mailing list was large enough for him to hire a marketing expert so that he could expect a financial miracle by the third week of every month, Jesus showed up. Does this mess up everything for John? NO! John was the voice of God, not the voice of man. When men are truly speaking for God, His presence only enhances things. When they speak for themselves, the presence of the Lord throws them into a quandary. It messes up their long-term goals of greatness.

If Jesus were walking the earth today, He would have lots of competition. He would encounter many "ministries" that would be genuinely upset that His voice was taking away theirs. It's very evident that many ministries today do not agree with the voice of God. Hence, they do not speak His words. They have a message of compromise; it contains no repentance or call to holiness.

John rejoiced in hearing the voice of the bridegroom. He rejoiced in giving up his voice. He said, in essence, "This is great — now I don't have to have center stage. I can continue to get smaller and smaller so that He can continue to get larger and larger." I remember a quote from Rex Andrews, which said, "We must get so small that when we go through the eye of a needle there is plenty of room on either side."

Getting small is part of what I mean by rejecting the philosophies of this world. One of the great struggles Christians have is that of doing something great for God without letting the world know. Who wants to do spiritual things without others observing our supposed "closeness to God?" The true voice of the Lord will allow no self-glory.

In Matthew 20:20–21 we read:

> Then the mother of the sons of Zebedee came to Him with her sons, bowing down, and making a request of Him. And He said to her, "What do you

wish?" She said to Him, "Command that in Your kingdom these two sons of mine may sit, one on Your right and one on Your left" (NASB).

In this account, we see the "I want to be the one" spirit. In this case, it was a mom making the request for her sons. She wanted the world to see the spirituality of her sons. Closeness to God is spirituality; however, closeness to God produces humility, not pride.

Look at what happened when the other disciples found out about this request. In Matthew 20:24 we continue:

And hearing this, the ten became indignant with the two brothers (NASB).

Were they indignant because they bothered Jesus with such trivial matters, or were they upset because the two brothers were aggressively going after the positions the other disciples wanted? I believe it was the latter. This is why Jesus then gives them one of the great lessons in the New Testament.

In Matthew 20:25–27 we read:

But Jesus called them to Himself, and said, "You know that the rulers of the Gentiles lord it over them, and their great men exercise authority over them. It is not so among you, but whoever wishes to become great among you shall be your servant, and whoever wishes to be first among you shall be your slave" (NASB).

JUST A FRIEND

The friend of the bridegroom stands and hears and rejoices. John could have approached Jesus and said, "You know, Lord, I lived a separated life just for You. I preached Your words prior to Your coming on the scene. I even baptized You! That should count for something! Do You think I could sit at Your right hand in Your kingdom?"

John didn't do that. John's separation had developed a humility that would not allow any exaltation. John's own words were, ". . . the friend of the bridegroom, who stands and hears him, rejoices greatly because of the bridegroom's voice" (John 3:29; NASB). John was content just being a friend of Christ. John seems to be the type of person that would be content with others seeing only Jesus.

I can just imagine seeing John the Baptist standing with the multitudes worshiping Jesus during that great day in the future when every knee shall bow and every tongue confess that He is Lord. But John is not up on the platform. He is not seated with the other dignitaries; he's out in the crowd. He may not even be visible to Jesus. He's bowed down with his face to the ground, his eyes filled with tears of joy as he hears the voice of the bridegroom. He rejoices in hearing His voice. He turns to those around him and says, "Do you hear His voice? Isn't it the most beautiful voice you have ever heard?" Jesus has increased — John has decreased. That is to be the way of our life.

He Stands

"The friend of the bridegroom, who stands. . . ." Could you be content with just being a friend of the bridegroom? In Ephesians 6:13–14 we are instructed:

> Therefore, take up the full armor of God, that you may be able to resist in the evil day, and having done everything, to *stand* firm. *Stand* firm therefore, having girded your loins with truth, and having put on the breastplate of righteousness (NASB, emphasis added).

We are to fight the good fight of faith. We are to resist the devil. We are to take on the armor of God for the battle that lies before us. Having done that, we are now to stand. Stand as a friend of the bridegroom. Our lives are not to be filled with our activity but His. If we move, we move because He instructs us. Until He instructs, we just stand.

He Hears

The friend of the bridegroom hears His voice. "The friend of the bridegroom, who stands and hears. . . ." Because the true friend has ceased from his own activity, he is able, through his standing, to hear. The friend does not speak of himself; he only speaks what he hears the bridegroom say. Thus, he rejoices in what he hears because it is the true words of the groom himself. Standing is a separation. Doing nothing because God has asked you to be still, when you could do something, separates you from others. Separation brings revelation, hence hearing. When we speak what we hear Him say to us, we speak for God.

I Can Do Nothing

In John 5:19, the very Son of God teaches us an important lesson:

> Jesus therefore answered and was saying to them, "Truly, truly, I say to you, the Son can do nothing of Himself, unless it is something He sees the Father doing; for whatever the Father does, these things the Son also does in like manner" (NASB).

The Son of God took no glory away from the Father. He didn't boast of His own ability. He did only what the Father did. He spoke only what He heard the Father speak. He humbled himself and became obedient even unto death. His humility and obedience is what enabled Him to stand, hear, see, and rejoice, in the Father's direction.

If only we had that kind of humility. Just think what could be done for God if we lived with the kind of humility that would not allow us to even think about disobedience to God. What would happen in our world if men walked in such humility that the "I-want-to-be-the-one" spirit had no place in our hearts.

CHAPTER 7

FIRED UP!

WHERE WOULD JESUS WORSHIP? Would Jesus worship in a church that has no fire, or no spiritual desires? Would He worship in a church that is complacent about the lost?

Ron writes: "I stood in my pulpit and told my people, 'You need to fire me,' "

"You said what!" I exclaimed.

The pastor continued, "I told my people they need to fire me."

The events that led to this statement will help us to understand what this pastor was getting at. I had flown into the Minneapolis International Airport about an hour earlier and was being driven by the pastor to his church about two hours north of the Twin Cities. During the drive we began talking about the Holy Spirit and our need for His influence in our

WHERE
WOULD
JESUS
WORSHIP?

lives. For some time God had been renewing in my spirit, my need to fan into flame the gift of God that is within me.

In 2 Timothy 1:6 we read:

> For this reason I remind you to fan into flame [stir up] the gift of God, which is in you through the laying on of my hands.

After the pastor and I had talked about this for a few moments, he told me that he was in his pulpit when he told his congregation that he should be fired. He said to them, "I want you to pray for me until I get fired up." I agree. Not just for this pastor, but for myself also. I need to be "fired up." From what I have seen recently in our pulpits, most of our pastors and evangelists need to be fired up also. When this pastor asked his congregation to fire him up, he was expressing the same type of thing the prophet was in Isaiah 62:6–7:

> On your walls, O Jerusalem, I have appointed watchmen; All day and all night they will never keep silent. You who remind the LORD, take no rest for yourselves; And give Him no rest until He establishes And makes Jerusalem a praise in the earth (NASB).

God has appointed watchmen who not only take very little rest, but they give Him no rest either. We need this same "never-say-die" attitude among our pastors and congregants today.

We need to be fired up. We have become lazy. We make so much money and have such nice cars that we can't be prodded into denying ourselves anymore. Today's watchmen are taking a break and, in essence, saying to God, "Feel free to back off a little so we can enjoy the finer things in life." We may be very busy about the work of God, but we have completely relaxed when it comes to pursuing the God of the work.

John Hyde (Praying Hyde), the former missionary to India, once had a physical examination. Upon taking an x-ray of his chest the doctor found that his heart had actually turned around and shifted to the right side of his body. The doctor looked at him and said, "What ever it is you are doing you had better stop or you will not live much longer." At that time in his life John Hyde was leading an average of four people to the Lord every day, and spending hours in prayer. All John Hyde was doing was working for God. He had the spirit of the watchman, which says, "Take no rest for yourself and give God no rest."

The Holy Spirit was given to assist us in this endeavor. We receive power after the Holy Spirit comes upon us. This is a power to be what we cannot be on our own. This is the same power the Pentecostal church once displayed to a lost world. We were men and women of the Spirit, filled with the power and presence of God. Today, at least in America, we are men and women of fashion, filled with the latest toys the world has to offer. We don't pray, we play. Fasting is a thing of the past. Relativity has replaced revival.

Divers Tongues

Sometimes I wonder if we even remember what the primary Pentecostal distinctive is. It's speaking in tongues. The baptism of the Holy Spirit is what the great Pentecostal movement was built upon. Do you remember that? Do you remember when speaking in tongues was the primary message of the Pentecostal church?

Some people say that the reason the Pentecostal church does not deal with this subject as much as it once did is because we overdid it. All you ever heard from our pulpits was the need for everyone to speak in tongues. I don't necessarily disagree with that, but we seem to have gone to the other extreme today. If you compare how often our preachers addressed this issue in the past to how often they address it today, the pattern being established is not hard to see. If the current trend continues, within just a few years we will be hard pressed to find Pentecostal pastors who ever preach on the subject.

God began to put me back on track after a pastor asked me to teach a series on the Holy Spirit. I told him I would be glad to do it, and then remembered I didn't know anything about the Holy Spirit aside from the fact that, several years ago, I received the baptism and that I still spoke in other tongues periodically. That was about the extent of my experience. I refer to myself as a Pentecostal because of that experience. I'm ordained as a Pentecostal preacher. I pastor a Pentecostal (Assemblies of God) church. I must be a Pentecostal. Is that all there is to it? No! There is much more.

I remember speaking in a church where the pastor really impressed me. This particular pastor had a constant emphasis on the baptism of the Holy Spirit. When a person got saved in his church he immediately prayed for them to speak in tongues. His church was filled with fired-up young people because of this experience. Families were being restored, people were being healed, and lives were changing. Being in his church reminded me of how my home church was back in the 1970s when speaking in tongues and the power of the Holy Spirit was the focal point of the church.

I once watched a special on TV about the church in America. The report, called "In the Name of God," began by taking a look at a very successful mega-church. Pastors and laymen were striving enthusiastically to recreate their own churches in its image.

When the pastor of this much-admired church was asked why he didn't have a cross in his church his response was, in essence, "I find it very difficult to find one particular symbol that represents all that Christ means."

That astounded me! What he probably should have said was that the cross does not make for good marketing. The report then went from this church to a Pentecostal/charismatic church to interview those involved in a "laughing revival."

It seems that the "hot" churches today either offer Madison Avenue marketing techniques or wild and strange manifestations of the Holy Spirit. Whatever happened to churches that simply preach the gospel, pray for the sick, counsel the hurting, and care for the needy? Those things describe the essence of the church filled with the Spirit of God. I am amazed at what we have forgotten. We have forgotten that the baptism of the Holy Spirit is what separated us from other churches.

It seems today that we have completely forgotten our roots and are desperately trying to find out the secret for the success of churches that don't even believe in the power and ministry of the Holy Spirit.

When was the last time you heard your pastor preach on the baptism of the Holy Spirit? I don't mean when was the last time you heard him refer to it in a sermon. I mean when was the last time he preached on it with the intent of praying for those who don't have it? Something has gone wrong in the Pentecostal church today. We have forgotten the importance of this wonderful gift from God.

> My message and my preaching were not with
> wise and persuasive words, but with a demonstration
> of the Spirit's power (1 Cor. 2:4).

When was the last time you saw a demonstration of the Spirit's power in your church? It seems that we have shied away from praying for people to receive this gift because of how bad it makes the preacher look when people don't receive it. We have put so much pressure on the pastor to perform that it looks like he lacks faith if he calls people to the altar to receive this gift and then finds that no one actually prays in tongues. It's because of this that many pastor friends of mine have almost completely stopped asking people to come forward to be prayed for. Subsequently, we have many "Pentecostal" churches today filled with people that don't even realize what their church believes.

I once preached in an Assemblies of God church on the baptism of the Holy Spirit with the evidence of speaking in tongues, and found out later that two families left the church because of that message. They both said, in essence, "If we had known that our church believed this, we would have left a long time ago." These families had been a part of that church for many months without even knowing it was Pentecostal.

When I received this gift, I had prayed for it for some time and at many different times. If I came forward to be prayed for, I didn't consider my pastor a failure if I didn't receive. This was completely between God and I and the things He was trying to do in my life.

There are two ways we have compensated for the lack of people receiving the baptism of the Holy Spirit. First of all, we have simply stopped praying for people to receive so that we don't look so bad. The second thing is that we have developed a lot of theology that says you really don't need to actually speak in other tongues. You can be baptized without any evidence at all. I don't intend to argue that point. However, I would like to say one thing. Regardless of your theology on the baptism of the Holy Spirit, there is no substitute for people being so overwhelmed by the Spirit of God that they speak in other tongues.

A Word to Pastors

When I first started reading Leonard Ravenhill (now deceased), I got a little upset with what I considered to be his constant badgering of pastors. A regular theme through all of his writings is, "The problem with the church is its shepherds." At first I felt he needed to give us a break. However, that was before I started praying. After I began to give myself to seeking God, my perspective changed. Now I see all through the Bible that God's word to the prophets was to tell the shepherds that they were misleading His people. Though you can find instances of God rebuking the people themselves, a corrective word to the shepherds is far more frequent.

I was ministering in a church once when the pastor shared with me an experience he had. He was once involved in a discussion about granting credentials to prospective preachers. After some time of discussing this issue strictly from an educational perspective and whether or not they qualified academically, my friend rose to the floor and challenged some of their thinking. He said, in essence, "I believe we are looking at this from a totally incorrect perspective. We shouldn't be asking our ministerial candidates how much education they have. We should be asking them questions like, 'When was the last time you prayed with someone for salvation?' 'When was the last time you prayed for a physical healing and watched it happen?' 'When was the last time you prayed for someone to receive the baptism of the Holy Spirit and observed them speaking in tongues?' " I agree totally with my friend. We are asking the wrong questions.

In David McCasland's book *Oswald Chambers — Abandoned to God,* he cites an incident in Oswald's life when he was taking his Bible training. Chambers, who is known best for his devotional *My Utmost for His Highest,* went to a very small Bible college in Dunoon, Scotland, called "The Gospel Training College." Duncan MacGregor started this school. MacGregor was dissatisfied with the conventional academic approach to ministerial training. On his own, he assembled a few students, set up some chairs in his small church vestry, and began to teach them from his heart and life.

MacGregor believed that in most colleges and universities an intellectually antagonistic atmosphere retarded, rather than encouraged, spiritual growth. Even in seminaries, he felt that the purely academic approach stifled men instead of igniting them for effective service. "In ministerial training, there should be less of the factory and more of the garden," MacGregor said.

"My aim," he said, "is not sending forth ministers, but men with prophetic fire — men who cry, 'Give us souls, or we die!' "

I believe we need "fired-up" pastors. I watch many pastors around the altars of their own church praying for God to allow something to happen in their church. They, in essence, are praying for revival. However, they are completely removing themselves from the picture. They are saying, "God, let something happen here in spite of me." What they fail to remember is that in the past things happened because of the pastors, not in spite of them. Things happened because they were filled with prophetic fire. They weren't wimpy, they weren't trendy; they were, however, consumed with their God. They were men and women of prayer and power. Instead of becoming that, today we are hoping God will do "something" in spite of us.

THE RABBIT TEST

Do you pass the rabbit test? Are you pregnant with the need to give birth to souls? I once had lunch with Missionary Ray Pollnow from Spain. Ray is the founder of Centro Reto, a drug rehab ministry with centers throughout Spain and many other countries in Eurasia. Ray began talking about the struggle to get people to continue to follow God all on their own. He said, "There seems to be something missing in peoples' experience with God today. It's almost as if we weren't there to lead them each step of the way, none of them would proceed on their own."

Then Ray shared a story he had heard years ago. It's a story about a young boy from the south, sitting on the front porch of his house with his father. The boy had asked his father about commitment. Before his father could answer, a rabbit ran across the front yard. Their old hound dog perked up his ears, jumped to his feet, and started after the rabbit. You could hear his howling clear across the valley. Soon all the dogs from the valley joined in the chase.

After a while, some of the other dogs gave up, but the boy's dog was still chasing and howling. With time, all the other dogs had gone back to their own yards and were resting in the shade, but in the distance you could still hear the howling of the one who had seen the rabbit. There was no way he was going to give up. The first dog had actually seen the rabbit, the others had only heard about it.

When we think of the great men of God, they all have one thing in common. They all pass the rabbit test. They have all seen or experienced something firsthand that continues to motivate them, even after all the others have gone home. We used to call that experience the baptism of the Holy Spirit. Today we have "Pentecostal" preachers who never even preach on the subject and rarely even pray in their heavenly language. They need a fresh touch of God's spirit. They can only receive that through prayer.

CHAPTER 8

THE LEAST
OF THESE

WHERE WOULD JESUS WORSHIP? Would Jesus worship in a church which struggles with believing the full gospel and makes excuses for not receiving all He has for them?

Ron writes: We must keep in mind that "speaking in tongues" and what we call the "baptism of the Holy Spirit" are one in the same. There is a difference, however, in that the baptism is also a reference to the entire Spirit-filled life which includes speaking in tongues but can also include all the other supernatural gifts listed in 1 Corinthians 12. Many people try to justify the fact that they do not speak in tongues because this particular gift is listed as one of the least of the gifts. The following verse is often cited as a case in point.

And in the church God has appointed first of all apostles, second prophets, third teachers, then workers of miracles, also those having gifts of healing, those able to help others, those with gifts of administration, and those speaking in different kinds of tongues (1 Cor. 12:28).

They will also use Paul's admonition to desire spiritual gifts, and especially the gift of prophecy, as a justification for their lack of pursuit of the gift of tongues.

Follow the way of love and eagerly desire spiritual gifts, especially the gift of prophecy (1 Cor. 14:1).

Much of the confusion about tongues comes from failing to distinguish between the public and private use of tongues. Paul referred to his own experience in 1 Corinthians 14:18:

I thank God that I speak in tongues more than all of you.

This is a reference to his own personal use of this great gift. This is what Paul did in his private prayer closet. The Book of Jude states that the private use of this gift edifies the individual.

But you, dear friends, build yourselves up in your most holy faith and pray in the Holy Spirit (Jude 1:20).

There is nothing more edifying than knowing that when you use this gift during your prayer time that you are praying according to the will of God. "This is the confidence we have in approaching God: that if we ask anything according to his will, he hears us. And if we know that he hears us — whatever we ask — we know that we have what we asked of him" (1 John 5:14).

The gift of tongues also has a place in the public worship of His people.

> I would like every one of you to speak in tongues, but I would rather have you prophesy. He who prophesies is greater than one who speaks in tongues, unless he interprets, so that the church may be edified (1 Cor. 14:5).

The baptism of the Holy Spirit is for everyone. Everyone has the ability to speak in a heavenly language if they would merely pursue it. However, when the Bible refers to the "gift of tongues," it often (not always) refers to the public use of tongues. This is where the Bible student has to distinguish the difference contextually, whether it's private use or public use. It's in reference to the public use of tongues that it is listed as the least beneficial gift to the church body. The only reason it's the least beneficial is because without an interpretation, no one knows what was said. This is exactly what Paul is getting at in 1 Corinthians 14:5:

I would like every one of you to speak in tongues, [the baptism is for everyone] but I would rather have you prophesy [public use of the gift]. He who prophesies is greater than one who speaks in tongues, unless he interprets, so that the church may be edified.

Continuing in 1 Corinthians, lets looks at verse 12:

So it is with you. Since you are eager to have spiritual gifts, try to excel in gifts that build up the church (1 Cor. 14:12).

Paul is a teacher; he is concerned about discipleship. In that light, he says, in essence, "Desire spiritual gifts, especially the gift of prophecy, because the one who prophesies edifies the whole church" (1 Cor. 14:1). So prophecy is greater than speaking in tongues unless there is an interpretation given to the message in tongues; then the public use of tongues is equal to the gift of prophecy because the whole body is edified. The issue is edification, not the value of a particular gift. If the public gift of tongues is followed by an interpretation then it is equal in value to prophecy.

Speaking Mysteries

For anyone who speaks in a tongue does not speak to men but to God. Indeed, no one understands him; he utters mysteries with his spirit (1 Cor. 14:2).

What could be more uplifting than to have a personal audience with the Lord himself? When you speak in tongues, you speak directly to God and you utter mysteries with your spirit. It's deep calling unto deep. This is why Paul writes about mysteries. Fourteen different times Paul writes about the mysteries of heaven. When your spirit utters mysteries with the Spirit of God, you eventually gain insight into them.

Isn't it interesting to think how people try to discern and enter into this realm without the practice of speaking in tongues! When you speak in tongues, you utter mysteries. The more you do that, the more these things become real to you or the more insight you gain into them. I think a lot of Paul's revelation into the mysteries of heaven comes from the practice of "praying in tongues more than all the others." There is something about exercising spiritually. When you do, you develop spiritual strength. No exercise, no strength.

A Beginning Point

Since some people believe that speaking in tongues is the least of the gifts, let's examine what it means to be the least of something. Often "the least" is a starting point. The man with the least seniority is the one who just started on the job. The person with the least amount of knowledge has typically just begun life. The person with the least amount of experience is the young one or the beginner. Speaking in tongues is the starting point for all the other gifts. There is nothing wrong with desiring the other gifts, but how are we going to come into those gifts without having received the least of the gifts?

NATURE IS OUR TEACHER

> Indeed, when Gentiles, who do not have the law, do by nature things required by the law, they are a law for themselves, even though they do not have the law (Rom. 2:14).

This verse teaches us that there is a natural flow to things. When the Gentiles, who didn't even know God, did by nature things required by the law, they were held accountable for their own salvation. God has put a nature within us that teaches us right from wrong. Knowing right from wrong becomes either a blessing or a curse, depending on what you do with it.

In the beginning, a person's sin is not held against them because they are too young to understand right from wrong. But when they reach the age of accountability, they then become a law unto themselves. In other words, they are now responsible for their own salvation. This all happens by nature. This is why Paul says, "Does not the very nature of things teach you . . . ?"

BY NATURE WE START WITH THE LEAST

Our nature cannot handle the most or the best initially. If we give a toddler a tricycle, he can make good use of it. If we give that same toddler a motorcycle, he will kill himself. Which of the two is the better gift? The least!

There are things about God that we are not prepared to handle. God could reveal things to us that would literally kill us. So by nature He starts us off with a little. After we have mastered the little, He gives us more.

THE WEDDING CEREMONY

The baptism of the Holy Spirit (speaking in tongues) is the least in the same way that the wedding ceremony is the least important part of a marriage. The wedding ceremony is certainly important while it is taking place. When you are in the midst of the ceremony there is nothing more important than that. That is why we put 100 weeks of preparation into a 30-minute ceremony. However, there is much more to being married than having gone through the ceremony. When we compare the wedding ceremony to the rest of the marriage — the wedding itself is almost nothing. I know of couples who have had elaborate ceremonies and rotten marriages — and couples who have had simple ceremonies and great marriages. Which is more important? The issue here is that you cannot enjoy any of the other benefits of being married until you are married.

The initial ceremony may not seem like it was very important 20 years after you are married, but if you had not experienced it you could never have developed in your relationship with your mate. Paul says:

> Therefore, my brothers, be eager to prophesy, and do not forbid speaking in tongues (1 Cor. 14:39).

What's Wrong with Being the Least?

First of all, the least hurts our pride. Tongues are the least, and we want the best! Who are we that we think we deserve the best? Some people will say, "We are the children of the King. That is why we deserve the best." Consider this: We are children of the King of kings and Lord of lords. Therefore, we should emulate our father. We should live the way He lived.

Our King was willing to become the least for us. We should, therefore, be willing to become the least among men so that others will see our King. If Jesus had not been willing to become the least among men He could never have revealed His father to us. We would not have eternal life today.

> Who, being in very nature God, did not consider equality with God something to be grasped, but made himself nothing, taking the very nature of a servant, being made in human likeness (Phil. 2:6–7).

We often consider equality with God as something to be grasped; Jesus didn't. Jesus was willing to become a servant, even to the point of death. From our lack of Christ-likeness we have come to believe we deserve the best. We want God-like qualities, and if we are going after the gifts, we want the best; we don't want the least.

Consider Christ's temptation in the desert:

Again, the devil took him to a very high mountain and showed him all the kingdoms of the world and their splendor. "All this I will give you," he said, "if you will bow down and worship me" (Matt. 4:8–9).

This is a revelation of the sinful nature. Our carnal nature wants others to worship us. We want to be perceived as spiritual. Many Christians will say in their heart, "If only I could be used by God in mighty ways, then people would see how close to God I am." There is a desire in the heart of man to be worshiped. Satan understands this and it is exactly why he tempted Jesus so. That is one of the concerns I have in regard to the gifts. Sometimes they are pursued simply because those who operate in them are perceived as being close to God. Understand this — being close to God is not the problem. Everyone should be close to God, but if our only objective is to get others to see how close to God we are, then we have a spirit of pride, and a proud man does not like the idea of having the least of anything. Truly spiritual men do not want to be perceived as spiritual. They have only one motive — they want you to see the Son of God and that is all.

BEING THE LEAST REQUIRES A SURRENDER

Jesus had to surrender to the will of His Father in order to become the least. Consider Paul, the most prolific writer in the New Testament. Through his writings, under the inspiration of the Holy Spirit, he has had a bigger impact on the Church, century after century, than any other sinner, saved by grace, in history. Yet he says of himself:

> For I am the least of the apostles and do not even deserve to be called an apostle, because I persecuted the church of God (1 Cor. 15:9).

What made Paul one of the greatest apostles ever? It was his recognition that he was nothing more than the least. "For he who is least among you all — he is the greatest," (Luke 9:48). Do you see it yet? There is nothing wrong with tongues being the least of the gifts, because in God's economy, the least is the most. The least is the best. With even the slightest spiritual understanding, we would seek this gift for ourselves. It is the way to a deeper relationship with Him, and not just because there is something magical about the gift but because of the spiritual frame of mind a person must be in to receive it.

CHAPTER 9

LIKE A
CHILD

WHERE WOULD JESUS WORSHIP? Would Jesus worship in a church which struggles with pride to the point that it cannot humble itself and become like a child?

> He called a little child and had him stand among them. And he said: "I tell you the truth, unless you change and become like little children, you will never enter the kingdom of heaven. Therefore, whoever humbles himself like this child is the greatest in the kingdom of heaven" (Matt. 18:2–4).

Ron writes: Jesus challenges us to be like children. However, we must understand that there is a difference between being like a child and being childlike. Childlikeness is not necessarily something that is to be exalted. Jesus wants us

to understand the qualities a child has and the freedom a child has to simply believe. Children don't complicate issues. Children don't know enough to complicate issues. The reason we become contrary to children is because we begin to think we know a lot, especially when it comes to the baptism of the Holy Spirit. If only we had the childlike ability to simply believe, life would be much easier for us. The baptism of the Holy Spirit must be accepted by faith. It must be accepted as simply as a child accepts something.

> And without faith it is impossible to please God, because anyone who comes to him must believe that he exists and that he rewards those who earnestly seek him (Heb. 11:6).

The whole issue of the baptism of the Holy Spirit is that it is not something that can be intellectually grasped. That presents us with our first problem in regard to this issue. This is one of the great differences between an adult and a child. The adult feels he needs to intellectually grasp something before he gives it either his approval or disapproval, whereas a child can simply be told something and believe it.

We cannot please God without faith, and yet faith requires a simple childlikeness. Faith demands a dying to self or dying to pride. Intellectualism is an exaltation of self. It is a dependence upon self. Receiving the baptism of the Holy Spirit requires an abandoning of pride. Some people try to assume a neutral position in regard to receiving the baptism or pursuing spiritual gifts. They have not been able to intellectually grasp the issue, but rather than taking a stand one way or the other they try to remain neutral so as to not offend God.

You cannot be neutral in the areas where the Word of God tells us to purposely seek something out. Anything that is not pursued is never gained. Did you take a neutral position concerning the gift of salvation? Have you ever known anyone who said, "I'm not sure about this 'gift of salvation' everybody is talking about so I am just neutral on it. If God wants me to have it He will give it to me but I'm not going to pursue it." I don't know that anybody could be saved with an attitude like that. Yet that is the attitude some people have about the baptism of the Holy Spirit, and they use their position to justify their lack of experience in this. We are to ask, seek, knock, and pursue.

Where this is concerned, we simply need to believe the Word of God. The Spirit of God, whether it's in reference to getting saved or being baptized in the Holy Spirit, has always been given in response to prayer.

MIND-DUMB ROBOTS

The gift of speaking in tongues, the gift of miracles, the gift of healing, words of wisdom, words of knowledge, and so forth, all come through faith. They cannot be attained through some mental assent, they must simply be received. Some might ask, "Doesn't that make us mind-dumb robots?" In one sense it may — in the same sense that a young child doesn't question the knowledge of its parent and simply believes what they tell them.

Is a child wise or foolish to obey its parents? When a child is young enough, they are, in some ways, simply responding in obedience to Mom and Dad. They really don't have anything figured out — they are simply obedient. Is it a wise child or a foolish child who obeys its parents?

We are nothing more than children of God. How many of us have God figured out? Receiving the baptism of the Holy Spirit comes down to whether or not we believe the Word of God, not whether or not we understand it.

SELF MUST BE REMOVED

I have heard teachers on this subject suggest that when you speak in tongues you receive the Holy Spirit. I don't agree with that perspective. We receive the Holy Spirit at salvation. Watchman Nee once suggested that the baptism is the release of the spirit that is already in us. His teaching is based on the following Scripture verses.

> I tell you the truth, unless a kernel of wheat falls to the ground and dies, it remains only a single seed. But if it dies, it produces many seeds. The man who loves his life will lose it, while the man who hates his life in this world will keep it for eternal life (John 12:24–25).

When the grain of wheat falls to the ground and dies, it bears much fruit. The grain of wheat represents the human soul and spirit. The spirit (the seed) is already within the shell but there is a hard outer casing around it. The outer shell represents our human nature or our intellect. At the time of salvation, we receive the Holy Spirit. The baptism of the Holy Spirit represents the dying of our human nature (cracking open of the hard outer shell) and the release of what is already within us.

When we talk about being used by God, or being filled with His Spirit, we are talking about emptying ourselves of self. Self gets in the way. Self always seeks glory. Self always wants recognition. You can hardly state a church problem that doesn't revolve around recognition. In order for the Spirit of God to flow through us, unhindered, self must be removed. Therefore, God has determined that only those who die to self-glory and intellectualism can be used by Him. In order for the Holy Spirit to flow through us, unhindered, self must be removed.

What makes a pipe effective? It's the fact that there is nothing inside of it. Its nothingness is what makes it effective. When a pipe is full, nothing can flow through it. When a pipe is empty, then it becomes a vessel that can bring a blessing to others.

THE KINGDOM OF GOD

The Scriptures teach us that one of the ways the baptism of the Holy Spirit strengthens us is through enlightening us in spiritual things or in things that pertain to the kingdom of God. It also gives us insight into the Scriptures.

Consider John 3:3:

> In reply Jesus declared, "I tell you the truth, no one can see the kingdom of God unless he is born again."

The Greek word for "see," in the above verse means "to know, behold, look on, or perceive." This verse is not referring to the fact that one day we will literally "see" the kingdom of God because we are born again. It means that unless you are born again you cannot understand, know, or perceive the kingdom of God here on earth. There is an enlightening that comes into the mind of the person who gives their life to God. They are now able to see what they could not see before.

When the Bible talks about the kingdom of God, it typically refers to it in two different ways.

1. One is the life to come:

> And if your eye causes you to sin, pluck it out. It is better for you to enter the kingdom of God with one eye than to have two eyes and be thrown into hell (Mark 9:47).

This verse is talking about entering into the kingdom of heaven and contrasting that to going to hell. So this is a reference to that life to come, the life after this life.

2. The other reference to the kingdom of God is the life we are to live today:

And he said to them, "I tell you the truth, some who are standing here will not taste death before they see the kingdom of God come with power" (Mark 9:1).

The kingdom of God exists within two realms. The most common term for it is "heaven." The other term, which is not used as much, is "the abundant life." Consider Paul's words in 1 Corinthians 2:9:

However, as it is written: "No eye has seen, no ear has heard, no mind has conceived what God has prepared for those who love him."

"What God has prepared for those who love him" is not a reference to the life to come but rather of the life God has for us now. However, this life can only be understood through the Spirit of God. It takes the Spirit of God to reveal these things to us.

THE PATHWAY

The baptism of the Holy Spirit is the pathway through the kingdom. He teaches us how to live in the Kingdom of God today. He is the one who guides us. The kingdom is spiritual. God manifests himself through the revelation of the character of God. The Scriptures teach us that without the baptism of the Spirit there tends to be a lack of discernment in the things of the Spirit. If we cannot discern, we cannot move through the kingdom. It is a spiritual kingdom. The next few verses bring this out.

The man without the Spirit does not accept the things that come from the Spirit of God, for they are foolishness to him, and he cannot understand them, because they are spiritually discerned. The spiritual man makes judgments about all things, but he himself is not subject to any man's judgment: "For who has known the mind of the Lord that he may instruct him?" But we have the mind of Christ. Brothers, I could not address you as spiritual but as worldly — mere infants in Christ (1 Cor. 2:14–3:1).

The carnal man does not pursue deeper things because it requires a death of self. So if we go back to the picture in John 12, about the grain of wheat — it must fall to the ground and die. Dying is the cracking open of the hard outer shell. If it cracks open, then the life that is within comes forth. However, the grain of wheat has the life even if it doesn't crack open. That is the picture of the carnal Christian — he does not pursue deeper things because of the death that is required. He allows his pride to control his life.

The grain of wheat that has died depicts the spiritual man. It has cracked open and now the life that was within comes forth. The difference between the carnal man and the spiritual man can also be the difference between the Christian who does not have the baptism and the one who does. I want to be careful here because I don't want to create the image that the one who speaks in tongues is spiritual and others are not.

I believe spirituality has to do with a person's heart passion more than anything else. However, if our hearts really do want God, and we really do want to obey God — then we should want to follow the Word of God when it tells us to pursue spiritual gifts. These gifts are for us. These gifts are our means of moving through the kingdom.

At the time of salvation, a person gains a limited understanding of the kingdom of God. When a person is born again, he gains insight into the need for men to repent of their sins. That tends to be the primary focus of those who are saved but not baptized in the Holy Spirit. In and of itself, salvation is of primary importance. However, the life of Christ is more than just the forgiveness of sin, in the same way that being married is more than having gone through the wedding ceremony.

Once people are married, they don't spend all their time remembering the wedding ceremony. There is more to being married than just the wedding ceremony. The wedding ceremony is very much like salvation. When a couple weds, the two become one, much like what happens at salvation between the new believer and Jesus. The wedding ceremony will always remain something special and even critical, but it has very little to do with the development of a great marriage.

If a couple is having marriage trouble they don't solve their problems by reconfirming that they were married. They don't say, "I don't know how we could be having problems — because we were married. I remember the day we were married, don't you remember it, honey? How could we be having problems — we are married."

That is not much different than a person saying, "How could I be having problems with my relationship with Christ — because I remember the day I was saved. I know I am saved — I wrote down the date of my salvation." There is more to a marriage than just reconfirming that fact that they got married. We need to come into fullness in our relationship with Christ. We need to know how to move about within the Kingdom. The Bible tells us to work out our salvation. We don't work to gain it because we already have it, but we are to work at it in the same way people that are married have to work out their relationship.

The non-Spirit-filled believer tends to focus on the wedding (getting people saved), while the Spirit-filled believers tend to focus on how to stay happily married (working out your salvation).

This is what the Book of Acts is getting at in chapter 18:24–26:

> Meanwhile a Jew named Apollos, a native of Alexandria, came to Ephesus. He was a learned man, with a thorough knowledge of the Scriptures. He had been instructed in the way of the Lord, and he spoke with great fervor and taught about Jesus accurately, though he knew only the baptism of John. He began to speak boldly in the synagogue. When

Priscilla and Aquila heard him, they invited him to their home and explained to him the way of God more adequately.

All he (Apollos) knew was the baptism of John. All he knew was to preach repentance. His entire focus was on getting people saved. Then Priscilla and Aquila explained to him the things of the Spirit (the way of God more adequately). He didn't lose his message of salvation; he gained more power to proclaim it because of the Spirit of God. The Scripture seems to infer that they led him into the baptism of the Spirit. Now he could not only get people married to Jesus, he could disciple them into how to be good mates.

Consider Paul's words in Acts 19:1–6:

> While Apollos was at Corinth, Paul took the road through the interior and arrived at Ephesus. There he found some disciples and asked them, "Did you receive the Holy Spirit when you believed?" They answered, "No, we have not even heard that there is a Holy Spirit." So Paul asked, "Then what baptism did you receive?" "John's baptism," they replied. Paul said, "John's baptism was a baptism of repentance. He told the people to believe in the one coming after him, that is, in Jesus." On hearing this, they were baptized into the name of the Lord Jesus. When Paul placed his hands on them, the Holy Spirit came on them, and they spoke in tongues and prophesied.

It seems that Jesus was often talking to His disciples about spiritual things, which they did not understand. He referred to His death many times, and yet it constantly seemed to go over their heads.

> "But I, when I am lifted up from the earth, will
> draw all men to myself." He said this to show the kind
> of death he was going to die (John 12:32–33).

Not only did this predict the type of death Jesus was going to go through (death on the Cross), it was also a prophesy of the Holy Spirit. Through His death men would be drawn. That which draws us to God is the Spirit of God.

What Jesus was saying to them was that it would take His own death in order for the Holy Spirit to come and that they themselves would need to go through a death (death of self) in order to receive it for themselves. Having received it, it would become a drawing agent in their own lives. We do not have much ability on our own to draw people to God.

I contend that much of the power we are looking for is wrong. We seem to be looking for a personal power that will ultimately draw attention to ourselves. The baptism is designed for those who want no self-exaltation at all. We still have a problem with seeing a spiritual kingdom because we're so preoccupied with a physical kingdom.

One of the reasons the disciples had a hard time understanding spiritual things is that they were carnal; Jesus was talking about things that had to be interpreted spiritually. They were under the impression that Jesus was going to build a physical kingdom. They saw his death as defeat because it meant the end of their dreams of a Messiah who would overthrow the Roman Empire and replace it with a physical kingdom. Their dream of a physical kingdom most likely included places of exaltation for each of them. This is evident from the account in Mark 10:35–37:

> Then James and John, the sons of Zebedee, came to him. "Teacher," they said, "we want you to do for us whatever we ask." "What do you want me to do for you?" he asked. They replied, "Let one of us sit at your right and the other at your left in your glory."

We still struggle with the death of Christ. We don't really struggle with what the Cross means for us. We are all happy about that because it means the forgiveness of our sins. However, His other death is what bothers us: His death to self. Suppose you are mad at someone and ready to put them in their place, when suddenly your hear God speak, "A soft answer will turn away wrath." Carnality would be bothered terribly by that.

Not only did the disciples struggle with the thought of His physical death, they struggled with His inwardness, also. Inwardness always reveals our desire for self-exaltation. The lowliness and humility of Christ is a problem to those who desire to be lifted up.

His physical death is the doorway into the kingdom of God. However, His death-to-self is the pathway through the kingdom. It is one thing to enter into a large building. It is quite another thing to know how to get around inside it. The entrance is the easy part. The entrance is based strictly upon a work Jesus did. However, getting around in the kingdom is dependent upon our continual dying to self.

Jesus did things in reverse order. He first came to earth to show us how to walk around in the kingdom of God. Then He showed us the entrance to it through His death. Once, having been asked by the Pharisees when the kingdom of God would come, Jesus replied:

> The kingdom of God does not come with your careful observation, nor will people say, "Here it is," or "There it is," because the kingdom of God is within you (Luke 17:20–21).

This is what confuses us. The kingdom of God is within us. So how do we live within this kingdom? The answer is: through His Spirit. The disciples had a hard time hearing these spiritual truths because they had a wrong focus. They could not see past the physical kingdom of God. They could not see beyond the size of the church. They could not see beyond pomp and circumstance. They could not see beyond themselves. This is what the baptism of the Spirit is meant to do. It's to cause us to see beyond ourselves. It's to cause us to see or perceive things spiritually.

But Jesus called the children to Him and said, "Let the little children come to me, and do not hinder them, for the kingdom of God belongs to such as these. I tell you the truth, anyone who will not receive the kingdom of God like a little child will never enter it" (Luke 18:16–17).

A child looks for no personal glory. They look for no personal power. They have a simple faith. That is how this gift must be received. You receive the kingdom of God, or the Spirit of God, like a little child.

LEARN FROM A HEALED MUTE!

Dean writes: Nowhere did I learn the lesson of childlikeness as well as in evangelistic crusades in Africa a number of years ago! As I have stated before, God has blessed us to see many miracles, but one in particular sticks out.

We had been in the bush in East Africa for three days of meetings, when on the third day we called all those who had been born again to come and receive the baptism in the Spirit. Some five hundred responded and as I prayed for Jesus to fill them, and the Holy Spirit came down in power on the field. All together, as if orchestrated by a heavenly conductor, these precious souls began to speak out in tongues. It was beautiful!

One man's peculiar behavior grabbed my attention. He resembled something between a bird flapping and a jackhammer in his behavior. He was loudly praying in his own heavenly language and, from all appearances, was thoroughly enjoying himself. I rejoiced in my heart with him, but thought no more of him until testimony time came. As I stepped to the side and gave way for one of the African pastors to come on the stage and ask for testimonies from the crowd, something happened that forever changed me.

Walking proudly to the stage came the man who had been behaving so strangely. As he approached, I noticed that the entire crowd, including the African pastor, was looking at him dumbfounded. A hush enveloped the entire crusade grounds. The man took the microphone and began to speak and his words had a profound effect I didn't understand. Indeed, my interpreter was so mesmerized that he was unable to tell me what was going on. That's when I heard a huge shout and loud praising as an elderly woman was shoved to the front of all those listening. She was overwhelmed with joy, and I was clueless!

When my interpreter came to his senses, he explained something I wish all Americans would learn. Here is what he told me that day so many years ago:

"Pastor, the man who came up on the stage is well known to all of us in this village. What has happened here are two great miracles! You see, he has been a mute for many years, and he came to testify about what God did for him. This man simply said this, 'As you all know, I was a mute, but three days ago I received Jesus as my Savior. When this white man told us that all who were saved should receive the baptism in God's Spirit, I was eager to receive it, but he told us that all who did would begin to speak in a new language called tongues. It saddened me, because I did not think I would be able to do this, as I was a mute. But I thought to myself that if God was able to raise this Jesus from the dead, surely He could give this Spirit to a man who was a mute. And He did! And I can speak now in two languages!' "

It was my turn to be dumbfounded. "Then who is the older woman?" I asked.

"Oh, this is the second miracle!" he exclaimed. "This woman was blind and as she heard the mute's testimony, Jesus opened her eyes and she desired to be saved!"

This story is absolutely true! I wonder if it ever could have happened in the present climate we have in America. I fear that the only thing we would have done was start a cell/support group to help the man cope with his muteness and hurt feelings that someone would tell him that being filled meant speaking in tongues. We are too mature, too reasoning, and too "grown-up" to believe these things. Or as one pastor told me, "We don't need these things anymore; they are only for the illiterate and the poor."

Can we get back to childlike faith? The mute received because he had a simple belief: God raises the dead, He does miracles, His character is trustworthy, and He should be able to handle my "issues." Isn't that what we should ultimately believe? The mute received more than just the baptism.

His miracle affected an unsaved blind woman. This is what Pentecost is all about!

God wants us to go back to that childlike wonder and sense of awe that characterized the early church. Though our intellects and emotions trouble us, we will see God's power manifested and His church swell with truly saved and sanctified souls.

> And everyone kept feeling a sense of awe; and many wonders and signs were taking place through the apostles (Acts 2:43–44; NASB).

> The apostles performed many miraculous signs and wonders among the people. And all the believers used to meet together in Solomon's Colonnade. No one else dared join them, even though they were highly regarded by the people. Nevertheless, more and more men and women believed in the Lord and were added to their number. As a result, people brought the sick into the streets and laid them on beds and mats so that at least Peter's shadow might fall on some of them as he passed by (Acts 5:12–15).

CHAPTER 10

THE PRESENCE
AND THE BAPTISM

WHERE WOULD JESUS WORSHIP? Would Jesus worship in a church which struggles with His manifest presence and in fact works against it?

Dean writes: Perhaps the greatest underlying issue that brings the Pentecostal church in America to its fixation on the seeker-friendly methodology rather than on a dependence on Jesus, godliness, and the power of prayer in the Spirit is the lack of true spiritual revival. We need a revival of the presence and the baptism in the Spirit.

> Then Aaron lifted his hands towards the people and blessed them. And having sacrificed the sin offering, the burnt offering and the fellowship offering, he stepped down. Moses and Aaron then went into the Tent of Meeting. When they came out,

they blessed the people; and the glory of the LORD appeared to all the people. Fire came out from the presence of the LORD and consumed the burnt offering and the fat portions on the altar. And when all the people saw it, they shouted for joy and fell facedown (Lev. 9:22–24).

In this text we observe that which every person, whether they know it, admit it, or not, longs for. Indeed, we also see the process by which a human can gain that which is the only thing that can satisfy. I am speaking about "presence," meaning the undeniable, unmistakable presence of the living God! If we would learn the lesson taught here, we could see the transformation of our nation. We see the reality of what the presence of the Lord accomplishes. Often, after long altar times in my services, pastors will tell me, "I can't believe my people remained as long as they did. They usually leave within five minutes of the benediction."

Why do people respond this way? Because we are not interested in how their day went or whether or not they are enjoying or even totally understanding what is happening. We are only interested in what Jesus thinks, knowing that if He is pleased, He will grace us with what we are desperate for: His presence! *When God's presence is in the house, church does not become drudgery or duty — it becomes a joyous sense of being. Prayer and work and ministry become as easy and effortless as breathing. You get lost in a sense of "otherworldliness." And people will linger for hours — even the lost and backslidden! Everyone gets a sense of how eternity will be.* I have seen this repeatedly throughout the years.

There is more to this. So hungry and desperate was Moses for the manifest presence of God that this is what transpires in Exodus 33:15–18:

> Then Moses said to him, "If your Presence does not go with us, do not send us up from here. How will anyone know that you are pleased with me and with your people unless you go with us? What else will distinguish me and your people from all the other people on the face of the earth?" And the LORD said to Moses, "I will do the very thing you have asked, because I am pleased with you and I know you by name." Then Moses said, "Now show me your glory."

This "glory" Moses wanted to see was the presence of God. The term used is the Hebrew word *kabod*, meaning "weightiness, or, abstractly, imposing presence." Why did Moses want this so? It's because the presence of God is THE distinguishing mark of the people of God. Without His miraculous presence, we are nothing and have nothing. This presence that can be felt and at times seen marks us as God's, and is a sign to this world of judgment and forgiveness. And it is addictive! See how Moses, who had already experienced it and seen the glory of God, begs like an addict, "Show me your glory!" Once a person has been in His presence, he or she can't get enough!

Why? Because in the presence of the Lord we are spoken to. In the presence of the Lord there is joy and pleasure forevermore. In the presence of the Lord we are hidden and kept safe. In the presence of the Lord all our spiritual battles are fought victoriously and our enemies are subdued. In the presence of the Lord all that the enemy has stolen and ripped off is returned to us and more is given besides! In the presence of the Lord we are given rest. (That's why those who wait on the Lord renew their strength.) In the presence of the Lord no enemy can stand against us. In the presence of the Lord our prayers are heard and answered.

Don't you see? It was the presence of God that split the Red Sea and defeated the Egyptians! It was the presence of God that gave the Children of God a cloud by day and pillar of fire by night to guide their steps. It was the presence of God that filled Solomon's temple upon its dedication so much so that the priests could not even stand to minister. It was the presence of God that came among us in the person of God's Son Jesus Christ that healed our sick, raised our dead, cast out our devils, and went to a Cross for our sins, setting us free forever from the fear of death and judgment.

It was the presence of God that came down upon those waiting disciples and clothed them in power and enabled them to speak in other tongues. Indeed, it was the presence of God that came down on Pentecost that brought spiritual awakening, conviction, and thousands of salvations.

It was and is the presence of God in His Spirit that fills and indwells the body of Christ, administers the kingdom of God, and that calls, equips, and appoints for service. It is only by the presence of God in His Spirit that people become more than church members — they become born again. They are not just prayed for; they are healed. They are not filled just with knowledge; they are filled with the Spirit and they speak in other tongues. They don't leave the same, they truly become new creations; old things pass away and all things become new. It isn't by church growth means, but rather by God's radical Spirit presence that every true advance of the Kingdom is made.

It is the presence of God that comes down when we gather in unity and it comes in the person of the Holy Spirit who is to us the spirit of truth, the spirit of witness, the spirit of conviction, the spirit of power, the spirit of holiness, the spirit of life, the spirit of adoption, the spirit of help, the spirit of liberty, the spirit of wisdom, the spirit of revelation, the spirit of promise, the spirit of love, the spirit of a sound mind, the spirit of grace, the spirit of glory, and the spirit of prophecy.

PRESENCE BY THE BAPTISM

His presence is what we want in our midst and the world so desperately needs! This presence comes by way of the baptism in the Holy Spirit. When people are baptized in the Spirit and begin to pray in other tongues, there is immediate presence! People feel God. That is what our congregations react to. As seen in Acts 2, when God's Spirit begins to move, people of all generations respond in one of two ways: they either ridicule or ask what about what they are experiencing or observing. This is where most pastors in America have brain freeze. We are under the mistaken notion that when God's Spirit moves, all is comfortable, but the biblical record doesn't demonstrate that! People can and do respond in positive and negative ways, but a negative response to what God is doing from hearts unwilling to learn or be stretched past their comfort levels should not determine what we do or what we allow God to do in our midst. As Smith Wigglesworth said so long ago, "We should be moved by what we believe and not by what we see!"

Because so many of our modern-day, third and fourth generation Pentecostal pastors have no personal experience as to the power of the baptism in the Spirit, or the power of praying daily in tongues, and since many have never truly been in His supernatural presence, they really can't stand against the negative responses they receive.

"I HAVE NEVER SEEN A DIFFERENCE IN 35 YEARS OF MINISTRY"

That was the statement I got from a pastor who really didn't believe that ministers like me were of much use to

God's kingdom today. The sad thing is, the minister who stated this belongs to the same Pentecostal denomination that I do, and was very clear and sure that in his 35 years of "Pentecostal ministry" he knew of no one who believed what I believe regarding the difference the Holy Spirit makes in one's life. In fact, he told me that in his opinion, the cause of all the miracles he knew were happening in our ministry was "a reflection of personality rather than reliance on God's presence." It is no wonder that he was taking his church down the popular road of church growth principles.

He was blind to what had been passed down to him. In the baptism in the Spirit we have the remedy for all the problems on this planet: a demonstration of a supernatural religion in radical love as the people of the divine presence walk forth from their hiding places and shout aloud on the rooftops what Jesus has told them to proclaim! This man of God merely reflected what our church culture today clearly demonstrates: confusion and powerlessness. These are inevitable when the wisdom and resources of this world are substituted for the presence and power of God. He had missed the point and didn't understand the process!

God Showed the Process to the Presence

In our text from Leviticus 9:22–24 we see a process. Aaron lifts his hands, a sign of worship and prayer, both actions signifying surrender. If we are to be a people of the presence and if we are to help others receive the baptism in the Spirit, we must make a decision right now that we will not just pay lip service to prayer and worship. We must devote ourselves completely to the pursuit of God through intercession, praise, and obedience to His commands. The greatest tragedy in this world is not unanswered prayer — it is unoffered prayer. Perhaps second worse is prayer offered in a detached manner! The same goes for worship. The only kind of prayer and praise owned by God is that which is done with fire! Passion and working up a sweat is the means by which revival comes and miracles happen and society is changed.

> The effective, fervent prayer of a righteous man avails much. Elijah was a man with a nature like ours and he prayed earnestly that it would not rain; and it did not rain on the land for three years and six months. And he prayed again, and the heaven gave rain, and the earth produced its fruit (James 5:16–18; NKJV).

The singular Greek word used for "effective and fervent" is the word *energeo*, which is where we get the English word "energetic." How can we expect God's presence, how can we expect God to send the rain of His Spirit, to produce fruit in the lives of those we minister to, if we go about praying with the same amount of enthusiasm we exhibit as when we go to the dentist?[1]

Most pastors don't pray people through to the baptism in the Spirit because they don't spend time praying passionately in the Spirit themselves. My wife, Carol, and I have prayed for almost one million people to be filled with God's Spirit in over 21 years of ministry all around the world. We have learned many lessons throughout the years, but the most important lesson I learned early on was the difference I saw between those who devote themselves to praying in the Spirit and those who don't.

Those who know our ministry know the challenge we give everywhere to those who have been filled and pray in tongues. We tell all to pray in the Spirit for at least one hour every day for 30 straight days and see the results in their life and ministry. Why do we ask people to do this? Because of the true axiom: if your prayer life is weak, your life is weak, your ministry is shallow and weak, and your converts are weak. Conversely, if your prayer life is strong, your life is strong, your ministry powerful and deep, and the converts are strong and lasting.

The Word of God tells us in Romans 8:26–27 that we are weak and don't know how to pray as we should, but the Holy Spirit helps us and intercedes through us. The Holy Spirit helps us through the gift of tongues! Praying in tongues daily is a sure-fire way to pray effectively and deepen our prayer lives so that the overflow of our strengthened lives will cause deep, supernatural ministry to people who will be supernaturally transformed.

A Pastor's Testimony

As one pastor shared with me some time ago, "Praying in tongues for several hours changed my ministry. I used to pray some before I preached, but I found myself praying barely five minutes before church service while I was spending almost an hour trying to make sure everything and everyone was going to flow 'right.' When you challenged us to pray in tongues and see the difference, I took you up on it. What I did was start by praying a half hour in tongues before I went into the sanctuary and then I worked my way up to at least an hour. I even began doing this before I did any 'ministry things.' The results have been amazing! I can honestly say that I felt the presence of God, but I knew that those listening could feel it, not so much because they listened more, but because *what I preached actually brought them to the altar*, and when they got to the altar, they actually received salvation, healing, deliverance, and even tongues! In my entire ministry, I had preached on the baptism, but had never once prayed for someone who actually got it. In fact, it got to the point where I didn't even want to preach on it. After accepting the challenge and actually doing it, so many started getting filled, that now I get invited to my friends' churches to pray for all their congregants who need to be filled!"

I know that this can be the testimony of all who read this! There is one more insight I would like to share in Leviticus 9. In verse 22 we see that we must first lift our hands, but then Aaron *stepped down*. It is time for all of us to step down off the throne of our hearts, humble ourselves, and let Jesus rule our lives. The time has come for complete surrender! This is so vital concerning Spirit-filled life and ministry. God will not share His glory with another, so every room in our hearts needs to be opened and laid bare before Him. No more hidden agendas. No more desire for position. No more self-reliance or reliance on man's methods. Self-dependence is a sure means to dam up the presence and fire of God seen so vividly in Leviticus 9, the Book of Acts, and elsewhere in the Bible.

It is time to stop asking, "God, use me," and to start asking, "God, make me usable." It is time to stop asking, "God, help me implement this," and to start asking, "God, fill me once again." It is time to step down, humble ourselves, and ask God to make us useful and not famous. It is time once again to elevate holiness above happiness and pray, "God, I'd rather die right than live wrong. I'd rather be viewed as foolish and have Your presence than have men's respect and nothing but people filling an auditorium."

A PASTOR'S APOLOGY

Several years ago, I found myself standing at the altar area of a fine church next to a pastor who did something that forever knitted my heart to his and solidified my impression of him as a humble, Christ-like servant of God. I believe what happened that day will bring home the point of this chapter to all who read it.

After watching one-half of his congregation begin to speak in other tongues for the first time at the conclusion of the Sunday morning service, he wept and apologized to his church. Here's what he said:

I want to ask you all to forgive me because I haven't been a godly shepherd to you. For years I have not spoken on or challenged you to be filled with God's Spirit. I acted this way because you intimidated me. I know some of you are very educated and have very high positions in our state and our community. But in being intimidated by you, I became a follower and not a leader. To see what God has done this morning, to see you receive what I always knew you needed but was afraid to speak to you about, breaks my heart. I promise you today that I will be the man God made me to be — your pastor, a shepherd of your souls, and your leader.

This pastor devoted himself to step down, as our text showed us, but he also dedicated himself to praying in the Spirit. Today, his wonderful congregation has grown exponentially in its influence in their region. May this be all of our prayer! May we all repent and humble ourselves as he did!

Endnotes

1. Apologies go to my wife, Carol, who is a dentist. Sorry, honey! Ironically, her favorite hymn is "Crown Him with Many Crowns."

CHAPTER 11

FOR THE UNBELIEVERS

WHERE WOULD JESUS WORSHIP? Would Jesus worship in a church which struggles with believing His Word, which believes that some of God's Word is not for today?

> Tongues, then, are a sign, not for believers but for unbelievers; prophecy, however, is for believers, not for unbelievers . . . (1 Cor. 14:22).

Dean writes: Somewhere we forgot what the Scriptures said! I have sat in on many church growth discussions and conferences where guru after guru stated that God does not reach people through outward manifestation. I have heard a number of these experts, many of them Pentecostal in background, also state that the Bible says we are not to speak in tongues in any public setting so that unbelievers will

WHERE WOULD JESUS WORSHIP?

not be offended and be turned away from Jesus. This is in direct contradiction to Jesus' command to all His followers that they would need the baptism in the Spirit (and with it, tongues) before they ever went out to accomplish His task of making disciples of the nations!

God uses tongues and other supernatural manifestations to get the attention of the masses of lost people around us, so that after they are sufficiently awakened from their sinful slumber, God's Word can then be preached and gain entrance into their unguarded hearts.

Too many have misinterpreted Paul's instructions in 1 Corinthians 14! Rather than telling us we shouldn't ever speak in tongues in front of others, it tells us that the gift of tongues was designed for unbelievers (see 1Corinthians 14:22). The simple point of Paul's instructions come down to this key phrase: *direction of speech*. If I am directing my speech toward people, they must understand what I am trying to communicate. If I speak a different language (like tongues) then I will need an interpreter. When I pray, even if others are present and listening in on my prayer, I am not directing my speech to them — I am speaking to God. When I am personally speaking to God, it does not matter whether others understand me or not. In fact, unbelievers (and unfortunately, many believers) generally don't understand prayer anyway. If I pray in a supernatural way (tongues) and people hear me, it will pique their conscience and curiosity, leaving them open to the convicting, saving power of the presence of God's Spirit. This is what happened when God first filled people with His Spirit in Acts 2. The disciples were filled in a public manner, unbelievers came, saw, and didn't understand, and yet, in their open state of heart, those unbelievers heard the Word preached after the fire and wind and tongues, and 3,000 were saved and baptized that day.

Many say, "The only way people were saved through tongues was because everyone heard the preaching of the gospel in their own language. They weren't speaking in anything but the languages of men." The next few paragraphs address this issue.

WHAT DOES THIS MEAN?

> And when the day of Pentecost had come, they were all together in one place. And suddenly there came from heaven a noise like a violent rushing wind, and it filled the whole house where they were sitting. And there appeared to them tongues as of fire distributing themselves, and they rested on each one of them. And they were all filled with the Holy Spirit and began to speak with other tongues, as the Spirit was giving them utterance (Acts 2:1–4; NAS95).

Ron writes: What if you were one of the 120 just waiting in the upper room? What if, after a while, you began to doubt the whole thing? What if you started being tempted while you sat there, and started having bad thoughts about those around you, when suddenly a noise came from heaven that literally shook the room. A violent rushing wind filled the whole house where you were sitting. And then just as suddenly you saw tongues of fire resting on the head of each person, including yourself. Would that change your life? Would that cause you to adjust your thinking away from temptation over to holiness? I think it would. Then what would happen if, when you were going to try to describe what you just witnessed with someone around you, and all you could do was speak in a language you never learned. What then?

The presence of God is meant to change us. An encounter with God is like nothing this world can offer us. This was a supernatural event. The church of Jesus Christ was birthed in the supernatural and it is meant to continue in the supernatural, but interestingly enough, this supernatural event was preceded by a prayer meeting. I once heard a preacher say, "God does the super, and we do the natural." We do what we can do. We can wait on God. We can pray. However, if we stop doing the natural, God will stop doing the super.

EACH ONE HEARING THEM SPEAK

I want us to consider just how supernatural this event really was. Obviously, the very fact that they were speaking in tongues was supernatural but there is another facet to this event that we don't often consider.

Now there were Jews living in Jerusalem, devout men, from every nation under heaven. And when this sound occurred, the multitude came together, and were bewildered, because they were each one hearing them speak in his own language. And they were amazed and marveled, saying, "Why, are not all these who are speaking Galileans? And how is it that we each hear them in our own language to which we were born?" (Acts 2:5–8; NASB).

They then go on to list all the different languages that were represented in the crowd. Here is what I want to propose. I don't believe they were merely hearing people speak in their native tongue. What would be so special about someone being bilingual or even trilingual? If that were the case the whole event could have been dismissed. There was something very different happening here. It's revealed in verse eight, *"We each hear them in our own language."* I don't believe one of them was speaking the language of the Medes, and another speaking the language of the Egyptians, and still another speaking the language of Rome, so that each foreign visitor could pick out the one speaking in his language — they each heard their own language coming out of the one man.

On my very first trip to Africa with Dean, he was telling me of a trip he had taken to Mexico once and how when the Holy Spirit would come upon him he would preach in tongues and the natives understood him. He doesn't speak Spanish but he does speak in tongues, and yet when he preached to them (in tongues) they understood him. His heavenly language is not Spanish. If any of you have ever been anywhere within a hundred yards of Dean while he is praying, you can hear him. He primarily prays in tongues. Rarely have I heard him pray in his own language. His gift of tongues is not in the form of the Spanish language.

One time, Dean and I and others were meeting for prayer before a church service. Dean was doing his usual thing — praying loudly and pacing back and forth. In the midst of the prayer time, a lady from our church stopped me while I was walking by and she said, "Do you hear Dean praying? He's praying in Spanish." She said, "I know Spanish and I hear him in Spanish." Dean was not praying in Spanish, yet she heard him in that language.

I believe that is one of the miracles of the Day of Pentecost. They each heard them in the language to which they were born. I think this is part of what 1 Corinthians 14:22 is getting at when it says, "Tongues are for the unbeliever." The fact that they each heard the same man in their own tongue is what convinced them that this had to be God. Why else do you think they said what they did in Acts 2:12?

> And they all continued in amazement and great perplexity, saying to one another, "What does this mean?"

This is why I don't buy into the argument which says only missionaries should use tongues and that God will give them the language of the group of people they are working with. God gives us the gift of tongues; that is all that is necessary. The Holy Spirit prays through us, and when He does, He translates for us. That's the miracle.

I have taught at pastors' schools in Africa, Spain, Hungary, and Portugal, and in each case, a person stood beside me while I was speaking and translated what I said into the language of those listening. That's not much different than what the Holy Spirit does when we speak in His language — he translates it into what the crowd needs to hear.

When Jesus left the earth, He said that it would be to our advantage for Him to go away so that the Comforter could come. One of the definitions of the Comforter is "one comes alongside." Isn't that an interesting thought that while they were speaking in tongues the Holy Spirit came alongside and translated what they were saying into the language of those listening?

A UNIQUE PHENOMENON IN OUR CRUSADES

Dean writes: In our crusades around the world, we used to follow a basic formula. We would preach the gospel and give an altar call for salvation. After we gathered in the souls the Lord graciously gave us, we then would preach a brief message on healing and ask all the sick to come forward. God would heal the blind, deaf, and lame, and more would be saved. Generally, on the third day of meetings we would gather all the new believers and teach them, in the crusade setting, on the baptism in the Spirit. We then would pray for the large crowds to be filled and God would graciously answer their cry to Him. But one day something happened that forever changed our ministry.

We were preaching a crusade in Uganda and many people were being saved, a large number of healings had transpired also. That's when I began to realize a dynamic that is very similar all over the world. Those in attendance could be divided into three groups: the very interested group that listened to every word, then the less interested group that comprised the fringe of the crowd, listening, but not paying as much attention as we would have liked, and then the skeptics who simply showed up because there was a crowd.

After about five days, I noticed that the less interested group became a little more interested as the sick were healed, while the skeptics really didn't seem to change much. As we gathered in souls and people came and testified about their healing, the crowds listened somewhat, but there was always unrest on the grounds — children playing, adults talking, etc. This occurred until the evening on the fifth day. That evening we preached on the baptism in the Holy Spirit and some 500 came forward.

I lifted my hands and prayed for the people to be filled and I looked over the crusade grounds as my prayer was being interpreted. I saw people walking, talking, children playing, and even the cows of a local herdsman grazing on the field. That's when it happened. I saw it with my own eyes! When the interpreter finished the prayer, God poured out His Spirit and the new believers drank in all He poured out and returned their thanks in new words never spoken before by their lips. No one on the grounds moved or spoke! They were gripped in a way I had never noticed. The nominal, the skeptics, all became speechless and even gathered up front to watch with hushed tones what was happening. After the sound of those being filled died down, the now entirely attentive crowd turned their eyes upon me and the interpreter, searching with their eyes and their hearts. My interpreter nudged me and I preached a brief salvation message and many of those who had not responded before now came running to Christ!

That's when it hit me! God did not use a healing or an effectively run crusade to establish the church and save the first souls. He used the baptism in the Holy Spirit and people praying in other tongues to attract new church members! We had been doing it all wrong for years! We thought we should wait until the end of the week to pray for the baptism, and I truly believe we didn't win as many souls as we could have! Now, we pray for the in-filling from the very beginning of all our crusades, no matter if it is in Africa or America, and we see more souls saved by far than we ever did before! We got back to the biblical pattern.

A True Story

Having been blessed to see so many amazing miracles of healing and so many filled with the Holy Spirit with the evidence of tongues through our ministry, we have had many things to rejoice with others about, but also many interesting encounters.

Some years back, I was preaching at an outreach of a Pentecostal group. Some 1,200 responded to the altar call for repentance. People were rejoicing and praising God for the mighty harvest! When over 1,000 were baptized in the Spirit, speaking in unknown tongues for the first time in their lives, and waves of God's glory were passing over all at the altar, I was "accosted" by a leader of the Pentecostal group that was putting on the outreach.

"I totally disagree with this!" he told me. "This is totally wrong! What if there is an unbeliever here? We should take these people to another room and do it privately. The main auditorium is not the place for this."

My response to him was this: "God is the One who filled them with His Spirit, not me. I think you will have to take that up with Him. Are you really trying to imply that God did it wrong when He first did this on the Day of Pentecost? It seems to me, that if we were really going to be biblical, we should do what they did and leave the auditorium and hit main street — just like in the Bible."

His response back was merely, "I don't *see* it that way."

What he meant, in essence, was that he had never seen that kind of outflow of power in his life and he didn't know how to process it in his mind. What he didn't realize was that it didn't need processing — an Aristotelian concept. It reflected God's character and behavior in the Scriptures. He simply needed to rejoice and embrace what God was doing.

This is in no way meant to imply that he was any less a man of God. He is a fine pastor and sincere believer, but his problem is the result of the church growth movement and its influence on the Pentecostal church.

I am afraid that we are as guilty as the Pharisees and synagogue leaders in the Gospels who were angry at Jesus for performing His miracles in the church and told the crowds there were other times and other places besides God's house to experience these things (see Matt. 12:9–13; Luke 13:14–17).

Isn't this the basic teaching of the seeker-sensitive church growth movement in America? Not much worship. No manifestations, only those things, which are easy to grasp and understand. And brief! Gone is the sense of majesty. Gone is the joy and awe of expectation in an all-powerful, omniscient God. What is left?

CHAPTER 12

GETTING PEOPLE FILLED

WHERE WOULD JESUS WORSHIP? Would Jesus worship in a church which refuses to understand and actually rejects the elementary truths of His Word?

Dean writes: Since I realize there are many reading this who have never prayed with someone successfully to be filled with God's Spirit, I wanted to share a few things I think are very important. Some of these things will review points already discussed.

DON'T SABOTAGE GOD'S WORK

The most prevalent thing I see that undermines people's effectiveness in praying others through to the baptism in the Spirit (outside of pastors themselves not praying in tongues regularly) is the way they set themselves up for failure. What I mean is this:

Have you ever said or heard someone say, "We are going to pray for you to be filled, but if you don't get it . . ."? No wonder they never see success!

In essence, they are saying, "I'm going to pray for you and you are probably not going to get it, so I need to apologize up front." That is nothing but double-mindedness! You will never receive any answer to prayer with that attitude! James 1:6–7 says you should ask without doubting if you expect to receive anything from the Lord. Furthermore, the Word of God declares in Luke 11:9–13:

> So I say to you: Ask and it will be given to you; seek and you will find; knock and the door will be opened to you. For everyone who asks receives; he who seeks finds; and to him who knocks, the door will be opened. Which of you fathers, if your son asks for a fish, will give him a snake instead? Or if he asks for an egg, will give him a scorpion? If you then, though you are evil, know how to give good gifts to your children, how *much more will your Father in heaven give the Holy Spirit to those who ask him!* (emphasis added).

This is a no-brainer! God promises that anyone who is born again can ask for the baptism in the Holy Spirit and receive it. That means anyone seeking it honestly and earnestly will get it through you as you pray for them, in faith.

If we want to be successful in praying for people to receive the in-filling, we must pray in faith, knowing beyond a doubt that it IS GOD'S WILL. I truly believe that when we pray, 90 percent of anything that happens, or does not happen, is based on our attitude. If we have a positive attitude of faith, we will see people receive!

People follow our lead — if we doubt, they doubt. If we are uncomfortable, they will pick up our discomfort. If we believe, they will believe and receive. God honors an attitude of faith; one that says, "God, Your promises are 'Yes' and 'Amen,' so I know this will happen." When I pray for people to get filled, I never speak anything but faith and direct their confidence in what God promises.

A Granny Receives

My wife, Carol, was speaking at a women's conference on the West Coast when a 90-year-old grandma was brought up to her. She had listened carefully to Carol's preaching and had come up to be filled with God's Spirit. A member for years at a Pentecostal church, she told Carol with tears in her eyes, "I never knew everyone could have this. No one told me that you could actually do this when you were prayed for."

Carol asked her, "Has no one ever prayed for you to receive?"

"Yes," she said, "but our pastor always told us that it was all up to God alone and that He might not give it. He said that God was honored by the asking, and that was what was important."

"Oh, no, no, no," my precious Carol told that woman. "Jesus says you WILL be filled, and you will speak in other tongues!" She laid her hands on this precious saint and she began to speak in a heavenly language immediately. So strongly did God move on her that she trembled and cried and prayed in unknown tongues for over an hour! How many years did her thirsty heart long for what was right there for her?

Pastors, it is time for you to go back to standing on, and boldly proclaiming, God's Word! Remember: God says He confirms His Word, not our opinions. He WILL confirm His Word if we will only share it with others. As one saint told me long ago, "Don't expect to reap it if you don't sow it!"

KEEP THINGS SIMPLE, UNDERSTANDABLE, KIND, BUT FIRM!

I like letting people know exactly what is going to happen and that "No" is not an option. It is always good to inform people what you are going to be doing, so I let them know several things:

1. I tell people that I will be calling them forward to the altar and surrounding them with other believers so that they don't feel alone and "on an island."

2. I tell those that come forward that I will have them lift their hands, close their eyes, and that we will be laying hands on them, and so they shouldn't "react" when they feel pressure on their head.

3. Most importantly, I always explain that I am going to say a prayer over them and lead them in a prayer. It is important to tell them this for a couple of reasons: a) I want everyone to hear a faith-filled prayer because faith is contagious and a bold prayer inspires others, and b) many people have never had an answer to prayer and the fact that you are praying and actually getting a miraculous response totally changes their lives. Oftentimes, it is at the very moment of their baptism in the Spirit that so many believers truly feel the love of God for the first time.

AN OVERVIEW

Below is a brief outline that reiterates some of what I have shared. It is part of what we use to train altar workers.

PRAYING FOR SOMEONE TO BE FILLED

Knowing that we must lead people to Christ and get them filled with the Holy Spirit, here are some practical points on helping people get filled:

- Share what the Bible says about the baptism in the Spirit. God confirms His Word, not our opinions.
- Explain that they WILL receive and NEVER give their faith an out — see James 1:6–8.
- Tell them that when you pray for them, they will be filled.

- Explain to them that they are to partner with God in this miracle, i.e., it is called speaking in tongues because they must speak. God will not force them to talk, and just talking in English will hinder their ability to speak in the Spirit.

- Lay your hands on them and say a prayer over them that asks God to fill them, rebuke fears, the devil, doubts, and bad past teachings, and releases them.

- Lead them in a prayer that causes them to speak in faith.

- After you finish praying together, tell them to lift their voice and speak!

- Watch them and make sure they are actually speaking. If they are talking in English, tell them to stop and to lift their voice in tongues with you. If they are not doing anything tell them they need to speak. If there are any other problems, seek out someone in the church who has been successful in the past in leading others into the baptism.

A Brief Example of Prayer

Finally, I would like to give you an example of the prayer I lead others in and the prayer I pray over them.

Prayer over the people: Dear Jesus, I thank You for Your presence here and Your desire to fill all these with Your Spirit. Right now I take authority over this moment and rebuke all demonic influence, all bad past influences and bad teaching, and I release these people into the fullness of Your Spirit. I thank You, Lord, that each of these *will be filled with Your Spirit and will begin to speak in other tongues just like You promised* and Your Word guarantees. In Your Name I pray, Amen!

Prayer with the people: Now I am going to ask you to repeat this after me. When we are done praying I am going to say to you, "Speak!" and when I do, I want you to lift your voices with us and begin to speak in the new language God *will* give you. Remember, God only gave you one mouth: you can't speak two languages simultaneously. So when I say, "Speak!" I want you to speak out in your new prayer language.

Repeat this with me: Dear Jesus, I thank You for saving me from my sins. I ask You now to fill me with Your Spirit as You promise in Your Word. As a child of God, I have made my decision and I will not be denied. I thank You that *right now* I will begin to pray in other tongues, just like they did in the Bible when You filled them. In Jesus name, Amen!

WEIRD IS FUN, NOT FATAL

In concluding this section, I want to make this observation and share a testimony. I have yet to be in a meeting when people are being filled with God's Spirit where there isn't some level of "weirdness" or what might be termed, "bizarre behavior." But let's face it! So many people come from different backgrounds that there are bound to be a variety of responses you will see. Some people cry. Some start shouting. Some laugh and start shaking. I once saw a man get filled and fall to the ground and start rolling like a bowling ball, as someone else was filled and "glued to the ground" and unable to move for almost 30 minutes.

The issue is this: Let God be God and let people be people! We can explain to those observing what is transpiring, just like Peter did in Acts after the initial believers were filled with God's Spirit. When a part of the crowd accused the early disciples of being drunk (in today's world, they would have told them, "you are acting like idiots"), you don't see the Apostles telling each other, "We shouldn't be doing this on Main Street. We need to teach this stuff in the Upper Room and keep it there. Maybe an afterglow service, late at night, on a weekend, in a remote location, in a soundproof room . . . maybe that would be better. These people are not going to join the church if we keep acting like this, in an uncivilized manner."

This is not what Peter and the others did! They turned people's questions into a platform for preaching, beginning with a declaration of what God was doing in their midst. They neither justified nor apologized for the behavior of the people, and 3,000 souls came to Christ!

I realize that the "church growth person" reading this may be saying to themselves, "Aha! They blew it. The crowds were more massive than just 3,000. They could have had a lot more people in their church if they had not been so strange." Perhaps you are right. Maybe God didn't do it right getting them out in public speaking in tongues and ultimately turning their world upside-down. The only proof we have that that was wrong is how after the last 20 or 30 years of modern marketing techniques, and various other church growth principles, we've lost America. The church in America is dying while we debate the validity of speaking in tongues and the power therein.

It is time for us Pentecostals to truly believe what we say we do, unapologetically, and enjoy even the unusual things that may come our way at times. Strange reactions to the presence of God and certain excesses are not signs of trouble, but rather signs of opportunities for growth and good teaching. As one person said, "What do you do with flakes? You pour milk on them! Give them the milk of the Word!"

If we become comfortable in our own services, no matter what may arise, the people around us will be comfortable. When we need to correct those that may be out of order, we will do so in a way that will let everyone know that there is freedom for all, and yet loving, firm boundaries God has set. This will create a powerful, family atmosphere that will produce a fear and love of Jesus.

A CHRISTIAN REFORMED MAN GETS FILLED

I had been in three days of meetings when a man approached me at the altar to talk. He was tall, handsome, very neatly dressed in a business suit, and extremely Dutch Reformed.

"Brother Dean," he intoned, "I was invited to these meetings and have come the last three days. I have observed all that is happening, which I must say is pretty 'out there.' We don't do these things in my church. But after having been here and having studied biblically what you spoke on, I have decided that all this is 'of God,' and I want it. However, I would like to be filled with the Spirit in a much more dignified manner."

Honestly, I had no idea what to do. How does one pray that someone receive anything in a "dignified manner"? I'm a Greek. We don't understand dignified. Loud, crazy, throw olives, light cheese on fire and sing: that I understand, but not "dignified." So I looked at him, smiled, said, "Okay," and put my hand on his head and prayed the way I do with everyone.

The last I saw that man, he was on the floor rolling from side to side with his clothes rumpled, hair disheveled, speaking in tongues, and laughing. He may still be there! When I saw him, I stepped over him and said, "I'm so glad you got it 'dignified,' brother."

Here is the moral to that story: it is time to be, as the Christian song says, "Undignified," and let God be God. God is good, and if we let Him do what He wants, the way He wants, how He wants, we will see exciting things happen that will transform people, no matter what their background may be.

A Tale of Two Fires

If we will not do things according to the Word and allow God to build His church through His Spirit but rather substitute our own ideas as to how to grow His church, then we will not only mislead the lost, giving them false hopes and a faith that will not sustain or save them, but we will also die ourselves.

> Aaron's sons Nadab and Abihu took their censers, put fire in them and added incense; and they offered unauthorized fire before the LORD, contrary to his command. So fire came out from the presence of the LORD and consumed them, and they died before the LORD. Moses then said to Aaron, "This is what the LORD spoke of when he said: "Among those who approach me I will show myself holy; in the sight of all the people I will be honored." Aaron remained silent (Lev. 10:1–3).

We cannot substitute man's fire for God's fire! When we eliminate God's Spirit we must substitute Him with something. Nadab and Abihu replaced Him with their own enthusiasm. They had just been ordained, God had just poured out His fire, and the people had responded: they probably felt good about themselves. However, they made a fatal mistake! They tried to improve on God's ways!

There is an incredible lesson to be learned from this story: God did not judge Nadab and Abihu on their motives — *He judged them because of their methodology.* Their motives may have been right, but God is concerned about the way things are done — and they did what God did not instruct. They had just witnessed God's fire in response to their strictly obeying His step-by-step instructions. You might say that, at least from God's perspective, the methodology is as sacred as the message.

We need Pentecost again! Man's efforts do not accomplish God's goals. It is far easier to excite people's passions than it is to kindle their souls. That which man's passion leaves behind are lost people with excited emotions and adrenaline, but not anointing!

We have become the leaders God prophesied against in Jeremiah 2:8:

> The priests did not ask, "Where is the LORD?"
> Those who deal with the law did not know me; the
> leaders rebelled against me. The prophets prophesied
> by Baal, following worthless idols.

We are not interested in where God's presence has gone, so long as people like us and attend our services. We keep asking how to get more people to church and God says, "Wrong question! You should wonder where I went because my glory left the sanctuary!" We have abandoned our prayer and Bible times where we would have received more infillings to reach the lost, and we did this to read the latest book or go to the latest seminar. This resulted in our "prophesying by Baal." Baal was the evil Canaanite god whose worship was very sensual. We have resorted to using sensual means to gather people rather than spiritual means that will save them. We put on the spiritual light show or concert. We have created a Las Vegas Jesus to satisfy the entertainment appetite, but we've lost the Jesus who gives food that causes people never to hunger or thirst again.

Satan has deceived us into abandoning the power God gave us to truly reach our world. He has caused us to lower God's standard regarding our duties and obligations to the world. The great commission did not ask us to build neat, relevant, coffee shop churches, and invite people to a nice cup of coffee and relevant vignette whenever they felt like coming. He said, "Go!" We are not to leave people alone in their "right to privacy" on their way to a living hell.

The baptism in the Spirit changes all this! Praying in tongues daily gives a loving but aggressive edge to our faith. It removes complacency from our walk and timidity from our manner (see the change in the apostle Peter after he was filled).

If we will spur people on to be filled and to be bold in praying out in their prayer language, we will see this generation of believers in America transform from receivers to givers. With the fire of Pentecost, we will seek out sinners to wake them up, turning them from darkness to light and from the dominion of Satan to God. Sinners are preoccupied, and they are in danger. We must knock, hammer, and burn God's Word into their hearts. We must take the blindfold of the devil off their eyes and let the Spirit move through us into them with desperate earnestness, intense persuasion, and fiery conviction. Let people hear us plead with God for their souls in other tongues, and if we cannot get tears to flow from our eyes, at least let people hear the tears in our voices as we plead with them and God for the sparing of their eternal soul.

When we are fully and freely "Pentecostal" in our church services and crusades, men's preoccupations are driven away and the subject of salvation is powerfully brought to their attention. Lost people need to be saved; they don't need membership in a Christian club. They need to be exposed to the all-powerful Creator of the universe and judge of their souls, not a powerless, timid church afraid to offend and ignorant of the things of the Spirit!

Indeed, Christians and leaders are, in my opinion, more to blame for not being revived and filled with the Spirit than lost sinners are for not being saved. God does not desire to improve the world. It is passing away with all its lusts! He wants to save people out of it, fill them with His Spirit and forge them into an instrument, awesome and holy, that will enforce His rule as they heal the sick, raise the dead, cleanse lepers, and cast out devils.

We need a new baptism in the Spirit and to be unashamed of God's working in us. We need more prayer meetings that freely speak in tongues and cause us to be filled with the Spirit so that we go out with power to reach the lost.

BOOKS BY RON AUCH

**PRAYER CAN CHANGE
YOUR MARRIAGE**
ISBN-13: 978-0-89221-118-0
ISBN-10: 0-89221-118-0
Paperback • $9.99
176 pages

Divorce statistics indicate that divorce happens just as much within the Church as in secular society. Prayer seminar teacher Ron Auch provides a solution to this rampant problem.

TAUGHT BY THE SPIRIT
ISBN-13: 978-0-89221-191-3
ISBN-10: 0-89221-191-1
Paperback • $9.99
232 pages

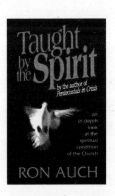

Although the Church is currently emphasizing warfare prayer and actively engaging in what is called spiritual battle, why is it that so little seems to be happening? Prayer seminar teacher Ron Auch has some strong answers.

*Available at Christian bookstores nationwide
or at www.newleafpress.net*

BOOKS BY RON AUCH

SWEPT AWAY BY HIS PRESENCE
ISBN-13: 978-0-89221-377-1
ISBN-10: 0-89221-377-9
Paperback • $11.99
160 pages

Prayer leader and seminar speaker Ron Auch shows us how laziness and indifference have ruined our prayer lives, to the extent that the Church is lacking power. Here is a convincing book, designed to lead Christians out of the doldrums. Originally titled *Pentecostals in Crisis*.

WHEN HE APPEARS
ISBN-13: 978-0-89221-498-3
ISBN-10: 0-89221-498-8
Paperback • $9.99
168 pages

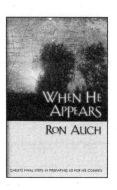

The Song of Solomon is probably one of the most enigmatic books of the Bible, yet this study by Ron Auch looks at this beautiful book as an allegory of Christ and His bride, the Church. An insightful and rich study of a lovely book.

Available at Christian bookstores nationwide
or at www.newleafpress.net